AN UNEXPECTED GRIEF

MOURNING THE DEATH OF AN EX-SPOUSE

EVELYN DAHLKE

Living Faith Publishing

ISBN: 978-0-578-24906-3

PRINTED IN THE UNITED STATES OF AMERICA

This book is dedicated
to all those
who have lost an ex-spouse or partner
and were unable to talk about it

Table of Contents

"Blessed are those who mourn . . .
for they will be comforted."

Luke 4:5

Foreword

THIS BOOK WRITTEN by Pastor Evelyn Dahlke is an interesting read. It was written following the death of her former spouse, Bob, a man to whom she had been married almost 24 years and from whom she had been divorced about as long. Her writing reveals the emotional pain, confusion, conflict and remarkable courage she found to re-engage in his final days. The book was constructed at the intersection of Pastor Evelyn's experience as a divorced woman whose husband dies, as a severely abused farm wife and as a Lutheran pastor whose heart of compassion wins out in the end.

This book has an interesting style and format. In some places it reads like a ship captain's log documenting the events of the day. In some parts it is like a memoir, a personal and painful telling of what it was like to be abused by the one with whom she had dreamed a farm into being and with whom she had brought three daughters into the world. In some places it reads like a sermon by one who feels called to use her experience to reach out to others. Pastor Evelyn uses her poetry to portray the rhythm and rhyme of her experience and thought. The author's voice is authentic, colloquial, and at times very raw.

There is something in this book for any number of readers. If you are walking through the illness and death of a loved one there is a lot about the nuances of dying, and death, burial and bereavement that could help you feel less alone. If you are a spiritual seeker there is an examination of some of the most difficult concepts, notions, and ideas that make up religious thought. For example, Pastor Evelyn wrestles with such theological questions as the meaning of grace, mercy, and forgiveness. For those who are interested in the impact of abuse and death on a family system there is plenty to consider. For those interested in exploring the intricacies of loss and grief there are both explanations and examples from the life of Pastor Evelyn and her family.

The book includes an appendix that provides grief models, in-depth descriptions of critical points along her journey such of the sale of the cattle. She shares her funeral sermon notes, a calendar of events around Bob's final days and the aftermath of his dying.

In total, this book is about Pastor Evelyn Dahlke's attempts to make sense of the death of the man she once loved, divorced and accompanied through his final days. It is true that she would have grieved in some way the death of the man she courted in high school and college and who was the father of her children but how was that different given the abuse, the divorce and her leaving the farm to become a pastor? In this book you will find one woman's struggle to make sense of it all. It is well worth the reading.

Janice Nadeau, PhD,
Licensed Psychologist and Family Therapist

Introduction

AT THE END of September in 2017, I buried my ex-husband. That followed a long month of trips to the hospital and surgeries following the diagnosis of a brain tumor. It was not exactly how I was planning to spend that autumn—with a death, a burial, and in grief. I wasn't planning to get tied into the life of a man I had divorced nineteen years earlier. But, when he called on me to help, I responded affirmatively. That response took me on his death journey and my grief journey, which followed.

Although in many ways my ex-husband and I were compatible, our marriage had been marked by his on-going abuse of me and by, what appeared to be, an on-going mental deterioration. We had owned a dairy farm together, which required hard, long hours of work. Between the farm's unrelenting workload, my fulltime teaching job, his battering behavior, and my call to ministry, I left. I divorced him three years later when it appeared obvious that who he was as a person and a farmer was not compatible with my new life in ministry. Yet, we had remained in occasional and sporadic contact through the years as he desired to be included in family events with our three daughters and their families. So, for him to call and ask for help did not come completely out of the blue. And my response of helping him was in keeping with who I am as a person, much less a pastor.

I had not thought to write this story until I was encouraged by one of my doctors, who is also trained as a hospital chaplain, with whom I had shared it. He felt the situation of the struggle I was having after I played a key part in my ex-husband's last month of life and then, my own journey through my feelings and thoughts as I struggled with a grief I didn't expect was important to share with other ex-spouses and partners, who may have experienced something similar but could not express it. My doctor felt it would not only benefit me to write but also benefit others by validating their grief experience following the death of someone that they had loved and with whom they had made a life at one time. It is with these thoughts in mind that I have written. Perhaps, as a pastor, I value human life even if I am not in agreement with how that life has been lived and how that life treated me. I am a person, though, first and foremost. It was me, the person, who believes in the value of all life, who took action when called upon.

My story takes us from pre-diagnosis, through treatment, to death, and the funeral following. It also chronicles the cleaning up and selling of the farm which he and I had owned together, a part of almost twenty-four years of my life. But it is more than that.

The death of my ex-spouse forced me to look at aspects of life and death from the vantage point of my faith, which I had never really considered before. What is forgiveness? What does it look like in a relationship of deep, unearned hurt? What is grace? How does grace inform the actions a person takes in life and even following a death? How did the abuse I suffered at my ex-husband's hands, the on-going, and at times, difficult relationship following the divorce, and his calling on me in the end for help complicate my grief? What did grief feel like for me as an ex-spouse? How do the thoughts of others, particularly on matters of forgiveness, grief, and grace, inform my thinking?

In the end, my ex-husband's death was a time of learning and growing I am not sure I could have experienced in any other way. The time since has been a time of clarifying my thoughts and attitudes surrounding death itself, especially in view of a complicated relationship. It has further refined my own knowledge of the grief process. It is said that we never really "move through" grief, but, rather, that we assimilate the loss. That assimilation changes us in ways as we move forward with our lives. What we learn in grieving becomes part of us as we ascend to a greater level of being who we are in living our own lives. That has certainly been true for me.

In one respect, this is my story. But, on another level, even though the circumstances may be different, it is the story of many, who have either lost an ex-spouse or partner as I did, or suffered another kind of loss, which had to be grieved. It is said that grief is the price we pay for having loved. But what would life be if we never dared to love? Grief presents us with the necessity of growing in ways we possibly would never grow otherwise.

If you have suffered grief in any form, I hope you find my story helpful. If you have lost an ex-spouse or partner and felt grief, thinking you were strange for doing so, may you find yourself in my story. In any case, may you be blessed in the reading of it.

Evelyn Dahlke

Death Drew Near

Death drew near
unrecognizable
slithering slowly,
clear as air
and
dark as lava,
into the sterile room,
with the intermittent beeping
of green and red and yellow lights
filling the stale space.

Heavy breaths hung
in your gurgling throat,
a sigh almost,
and chest rising once again.

Then silence
huge and deafening in its emptiness
with its mouth wide open,
the announcement
by the flat-lined monitor,
the moment
you were gone,
only the grayish-yellow butterfly
in the mellow, autumn sun
to mark your passing.
And, finally,
I am free.

You had to die
so I might live.

Evelyn Dahlke
March 19, 2018

One Last Hurrah

"DEAR RELATIVES, FRIENDS, Family, Co-Workers, and Brothers and Sisters in Christ: On behalf of my daughters and myself, we would like to thank you for being here today. It has been an unbelievably difficult couple of weeks for all, and the girls are glad of your support today." I had just climbed the four steps up to the chancel of the church, taken one more step into the pulpit, turned around to face the gathered congregation, and rested my hands on the smooth, sturdy, dark oak on the sides of the pulpit.

I continued, "Gathering at the time of a death is not only a tradition and ritual, but it is an opportunity to express grief, find some closure in order to reorganize and reframe life, and move forward," adding, "It is also our opportunity to formally commend Bob to God's care and keeping, and to proclaim the redemption and salvation granted to all of us through Jesus Christ, our Lord."

As a pastor, I had spoken these words or ones similar on multiple occasions during my twenty years in ministry. Sometimes I spoke them for total strangers at which times I struggled to find words that were fitting for the unknown person's send off. In those times, often the family of the deceased had met with me beforehand. When I had visited with them, they would help me discern what to say to honor their loved one.

Many times, the person had been a member of one of the

congregations which I had served over time for whom I now led the funeral. In those cases, I could draw on my own experiences of doing ministry with them, tidbits of personal stories they had shared with me, times when we had laughed or cried or were deeply serious in the content of our conversations. Then also, I often had been with them and their loved ones at the time of death, had read pertinent Bible verses and perhaps a psalm, and ended with a prayer. Those were easier and more meaningful funeral sermons for me, times when I felt my words and my steadiness of presence were badly needed and very much appreciated.

The funeral sermon I was preaching on this day, however, was both very much the same, and yet, entirely different. I was preaching this sermon for the funeral of my ex-husband, to whom I had no longer been married for almost twenty years. But why? I had wanted the duty, not as a pastor necessarily, but as one who had walked the final weeks of his life with him. Unlike the pastor of his church, who was fairly new and did not know him, I felt I was the one, who could best convey the message.

As the words flowed from my mouth, my thoughts were not on the familiar words I had spoken so many times before. Instead, I was thinking of the long line of people from the community, who filled the length of the church aisle during the time of Bob's visitation held immediately preceding the funeral service. I was thinking of the members of Bob's family, who had been part of my family also for twenty years before I had gotten the divorce. I was thinking of the conversations I had had with Bob's neighbors and friends as I separated from my girls and their families near the casket and made my way down the aisle greeting them. I thought of a few people, who were there, that I'd never met, assuming they were friends he had made after I had left. And I thought of my own relatives and my girls' in-laws, who were also there to show support.

"Jesus said, in God's Kingdom, there are many dwelling places. In some older versions 'dwelling places' is translated as 'mansions.' 'In my Father's house, there are many mansions'." (based on John 14:1-7)

I acknowledged the absence of mansions in the small, rural town of Arlington, Minnesota where Bob had made his life, but that, in the city in which I was now living, there were mansions so large a person could get lost in their many rooms. "Imagine mansions as numerous as the stars—room for Bob, room for you and me someday. . . all the outer space out there fits into God's realm—all the planets, stars, galaxies, black holes, everything we have discovered and all that we have no knowledge of as yet."

I also preached that I believed God's realm was right here among all of us people in our imperfection gathered in the sanctuary on that warm, sunny day at the end of September. "As we move our arms through the air, we may in some way be touching it, touching God's presence, even as we breathe the Spirit with each breath we take. We cannot fathom the size of God's love or God's care for us after death as well as in this life." I wanted people to fully acknowledge that God is not "up there" some place, but right here among them on this earth as they live their daily, human lives.

My thoughts during this time went to the volume of attendees filling the sanctuary. I felt surprise that so many people, who had come for the visitation, remained for the funeral. Many, of course, were Bob's immediate and extended family members remembering he had many nieces and nephews, many cousins. No wonder the voices heard in the opening hymn filled the large space! I also noted the facial expressions of the pall bearers, all recent friends in his life, their red and weeping eyes, the way they would rest their faces in their hands occasionally, even lifting a tissue now and then.

My thoughts turned back to the sermon I was preaching. I acknowledged that Bob's journey from "life" to "death" had been fairly quick, that people had just seen him alive a few weeks before, that his death came as a surprise to many. But it was not so for me. I noted, "I've heard comments that all of this went really quickly. For me, not really." And I went into some details of the past several months.

"He complained of constant headaches and a stiff neck." As I said this, I thought of his comment to me in early February. He said,

"I have a brain tumor like Joe," Joe the friend of his, who had had a cancerous brain tumor and had died a few years before. I had replied, "I doubt it. That would be very unlikely."

"When he rode with me to Baby Maggie's, one of our grand-daughters, first birthday at the end of April, he was having endurance and balance issues," I spoke. As the words flowed from my mouth, in my mind I saw the picture of him that day, swerving away from the passenger side of the car, then reaching back to balance himself on my car's side. I encouraged him that day, as well as numerous times throughout the summer, to seek medical help.

During this time, as a school bus driver, he was delivering sports teams to their practices and teachers to the destination of a training session several miles away. My fear, that I expressed to him, was that, if he didn't seek help, he could take a whole busload of kids down with him. In fact, among the many days he drove for sports practices, he told me that one morning a few days before, he had bled out of his nose, eyes, and mouth leaving blood on his bed pillow.

As he told me this, I asked, "Did you go to the doctor?"

"No, I went with friends to the nearby Fleet Supply," he responded.

As he told me that, I thought, "No, it's none of my business. We're not married anymore. It's his decision." But then I remembered my feeling of panic as I lay in bed that night. Pure panic shuddered through me as, in my mind, I saw a busload of school children careening off the road and tipping into the ditch. I remember that I called him the next morning, telling him, "If you don't see the doctor, I'm going to call your boss. You shouldn't be driving a school bus in your condition."

Continuing with the sermon, I spoke of forgiveness, citing the disciple Peter's question to Jesus at one point when they were traveling in ministry together.

Peter asked, "How many times are we to forgive someone who has wronged us; as many as seven times?"

Jesus answered, "As many as seven times seven (or seventy-seven times)," indicating that there should be no limit to our forgiveness of a person who has wronged us.

By speaking of forgiveness, I was acknowledging the human difficulty of doing this. Nevertheless, even as Jesus hung on the cross, he forgave those who had sentenced him to death.

I also proclaimed Bob's redemption, and God's gift of salvation to him. How could I even go to these topics in the sermon remembering the deep hurt to me inflicted by him, which had led to our divorce? Yet, I spoke of God's unmeasurable forgiveness, the promise given to Bob in baptism, of resurrection, and the gift of eternal life. Although I did not have a connection of love with Bob, there was some kind of connection—perhaps the connection of familiarity.

I explained to those gathered the events leading to his death, the long days within the very short time from diagnosis of his brain tumor to his death, and my involvement in that journey. It was that journey with him during those final weeks that led me to preach his funeral sermon on this day. For one thing, I was the only one who knew the journey from start to finish. I was sure people would want to know the contents of that journey. [APPENDIX I]

Also, the journey had become part of my journey by his asking my involvement in it and my agreeing to help. It is that journey with him from life into death and beyond that I acknowledge in the following chapters. Through my experience of taking his final journey with him, I acknowledge that, even after many years of no longer being married, I was still affected by his death. I was touched by it in a way I would have never imagined. Can it be that a divorcee will feel something at the death of a former spouse? What is the "something" that is felt? I only know how all of it has felt for me.

CHAPTER 2

The Butterfly That Met Me

THE MORNING OF September 30, 2017 dawned sunny and bright as only an early, fall day can with the leaves still green, the grass continuing to grow, and the summer flowers in the pots outside my porch door looking a little tired after months of vibrant growth. I was up and awake, showering and dressing before eight a.m. planning for the hour's drive from my condo in Edina, a suburb of Minneapolis, to the rural town of Arlington, Minnesota some sixty miles away. I had planned what I would wear for this day the day before choosing the black suit I had worn for so many important events throughout my active congregational ministry. I contemplated my clergy shirt, but I decided instead to wear a peach-colored, knit shirt with my favorite cross necklace. After all, I wasn't presiding at this funeral. By my request, I was merely preaching the sermon. Yes, I had planned the funeral service. I had chosen the hymns and the Bible texts. But the pastor at the church, whom I had just met for the first time the day of Bob's death, would be presiding.

I was out on the open road on time heading southwest into rural, farming country to the church Bob, I, and our three daughters had belonged to as a family. Although Bob was still a member there, he rarely, if ever, had attended for the last several years. As I drove the miles between my home and the church, I remember noticing how the crops were browning as they ripened, and that harvest time would not be far away. Although I had spent forty-three years of my life living the cycles of farm life, now that I lived in the city, I often forgot the natural changes of farm life throughout the year.

I arrived at the church by nine a.m., the first among the family to be there. Soon I was followed by Bob's and my three daughters, their husbands, and their young families. I greeted the mortician and his helper and proceeded up the aisle to see that the casket and the flower bouquets were placed appropriately. I took the three roses with the burlap bow bearing the golden lettering "father" out of the bud vase in which they rested and laid them on the closed portion of the casket's cover.

Then I proceeded to look at Bob's body to see how he had been prepared for viewing under the mortician's care. I can remember thinking that he looked very nice, very "young" to be in the casket. He was wearing one of his plaid, short-sleeved shirts, a shirt I had purchased some years earlier for him at a local thrift store. I had fixed the right corner of the chest pocket with a few hand stitches before delivering it to the mortuary as it had come loose having been worn many times. It was slightly bent over. His hands were folded on his stomach just above his buckled, brown, leather belt, which was strung through the loops of the well-worn blue jeans that I had washed for this purpose earlier in the week. The girls said they wanted to see him the way he always looked. That meant jeans and a button-down, short-sleeved, plaid shirt would be his funeral attire. As I viewed him, I noticed he had three fingers on his left hand that were not resting flat on the flattened fingers of his right hand. Instead, they were raised about a half inch above the others with his little finger standing up the highest. I thought, "Yes, even in death, he's defiant!"

By the time I had placed the roses, made my observations, greeted my grandchildren, spoken to the girls, and turned around, people were already parading in a line to view the casket and offer condolences. I talked a little too long with a few attendees, who mentioned some issues they were having in their lives. I guess I reacted to care for them pastorally because Bonnie, our oldest daughter, who was standing next to me, said, "Mom, you have to stop doing pastoral care. You're taking too long."

At that point I started walking down the aisle, greeting people, and getting hugs so as not to slow the line. Many of these people I had not seen or talked to for the twenty plus years since I had left the community. I purposely had chosen not to interfere with the people in Bob's life, giving him his space among relatives, neighbors, and friends.

When I had reached the end of the line, which extended into the entry of the church, instead of going back up to the casket, I headed into the fellowship hall to the side of the sanctuary where the pallbearers were gathered. I spoke to them briefly. Within minutes, the girls and their families joined us, the pastor led in prayer, and we lined up. As the opening hymn was sung, we filed into the front pews of the sanctuary, and the funeral was in progress.

The service was followed by lunch in the undercroft, a lunch for which I had chosen the menu along with two of the leaders of one of the women's circles. By the time the casket was loaded into the hearse and the family had paid last respects, most of those attending the funeral were already downstairs and beginning to eat. While I waited in line, I visited with some friends from town whose children had been in the same 4-H club as our girls and whose son had worked for us on our dairy farm for many years. Upon getting my lunch, I sat down at a table with my sister and her family and my aunt with whom I visited while eating.

It seemed like a very brief time before the funeral home crew was asking me to bring my car up into the line for the six-mile trip out to the cemetery near what had been our farm when we were married. As I drove following the hearse and the car with the pallbearers, the sun went behind the clouds and the air became humid. It was ushering in the rain, which was on its way for tomorrow. But, as late September days are apt to feel, it seemed balmy with a gentle breeze that lifted the fine hair on my cheeks.

As the pastor began to position herself next to the casket to lead the committal service, I happened to glance to my right under the frames of my glasses. I had noticed something that looked like a white, fuzzy, seed head on the right elbow of my black suit jacket. Instinctively, I simultaneously lifted my bent right arm and turned my head to the right to get a better look. Whatever it was that I had noticed on my clothing, I was still thinking the fuzzy to be a seed head, not so far-fetched in a rural cemetery in late September of the year. In the second it took me to take those insignificant actions, I observed that, what I had thought was a seed head, now had the shape of a butterfly. It had the distinctive dark outline of classic, butterfly-shaped wings. Yet, its coloring was muted, a grayish-yellowish-brown with no distinct separations as are usually seen on butterflies.

I had no time to study it in depth. As soon as my elbow was raised and I tried to focus on it more in depth, it took flight. Instinctively, I turned around to see if there were other butterflies from which it had broken loose. There were none. I scanned the area to see if there were flowers, which might have drawn this butterfly to my immediate area. There were none.

After that glance, I turned back to see that this one, lone butterfly was making its way through the group of people. It was fluttering the length of the casket—in a straight line from one end of the casket's cover to the other—only swerving to avoid a collision with the pastor's body as she took her place near the head end of the casket. The butterfly continued in that straight line, past the back row of tombstones, and into the evergreen trees that lined the cemetery's border. And just that quickly, the butterfly was gone.

With my mind on the strange appearance and, then, disappearance of the butterfly, the words of the committal service flew past me. Instinctively, I am sure I joined the group in praying the Lord's Prayer. But I was not thinking of the well-memorized words. What was this strange butterfly about? Why did it seem to form between the time I noticed a fuzzy shape on my elbow and clearly into a butterfly shape by the time I raised my elbow and turned my head? Why did it seem to form on my elbow and not on the elbow of another attendee? How could something that looked simply like a fuzzy, seed head on my elbow transform into the clear form of a butterfly in the split second that had just transpired? How come no one else commented on the strange sight? No one else acknowledged the sight of that butterfly. I couldn't help but think that there was some meaning to what I had just observed. It just didn't seem to be a pure coincidence. But what was the significance?

As I write this now, in my mind I can still see the butterfly traverse the length of the casket and flutter into the row of trees. The image is etched in my mind. I see it over and over again. And, I can't help but wonder about its meaning.

In the two-and-one half years since Bob's funeral, I have tried to brush off the image as simply a fluke—a weird, but insignificant happening, following a stress-filled couple of weeks. I have often wondered how that image changed shape so clearly as I simultaneously lifted my elbow and turned my focus in the image's direction. Or, did I just not focus on it clearly when it was resting on my elbow, and that focus was clearer by the time I had raised my elbow and turned my head to get a better look?

Since then, on more than one occasion, I have studied the designs on my shirts by looking under the frames of my glasses. The designs are clear and intelligible. So why was the butterfly not clear under the same type of circumstances? And, there is no argument by me that it truly was a butterfly as I clearly saw it flutter its way up the length of the casket and ahead into the trees.

It has been suggested to me that it was perhaps a moth because of its coloring. But I clearly saw the dark outline of the shape of its wings. It's simple existence in the situation at the time is, in part, baffling. Its peculiar behavior flying into and through the group of people gathered instead of away, the straight path it followed until it disappeared into the trees is even more baffling. Even the time of its occurrence has seemed like more than a coincidence. But, why me? Why on my jacket? Why in my vision? Why so obvious to me and to no one else?

I have had "unexplainable" experiences in my life before the experience of the butterfly at Bob's gravesite, experiences that have seemed to have supernatural elements. Perhaps, as an empath and a person of faith, I am more open to putting more credence on those experiences than another person might do. But, in my mind, the occurrence of the butterfly at that significant moment had to have meaning, especially since I had been the one to walk Bob's final journey with him. Although it had been a stressful couple of weeks, I did not feel stressed that day. I was aware—totally there—in the events of the day. All the difficult actions and decisions were behind me. I was mystified by this sign of life from what I felt was the other side of the grave. It was so direct, so unexpected, so unmistakable, it has left an impression in my memory which I carry with me to this day.

It may seem strange, but I have felt like the butterfly could have been from Bob—or Bob in another form. At first, I thought it was saying, "See what you've done to me!" Bob's emotional criticism of me, blaming me for everything bad that happened on and to our farm or cattle was an on-going feature of our marriage. It was one of the reasons why I had left. Within a second though, it seemed the message was more positive. It seemed to be Bob telling me that he was in another realm now. It was his way of saying goodbye and leaving the earth, "free"—and that he was pleased with the choices I and the girls had made regarding his funeral—that we had sent him off well. Finally, I thought it may have been a message from God: "Well done, good and faithful servant." Perhaps why I thought these things about the butterfly's meaning will become clearer as I explore my life and beliefs, Bob's and my relationship or lack thereof, and the circumstances of his death and my role during and after that.

CHAPTER **3**

Ashes to Ashes and Dust to Dust

AFTER THE EVENTS of the funeral, I and Bob's three daughters, Bonnie, Krista, and Amy, along with their husbands and families, headed to the farm place a half mile away, which was left in twenty years of disarray. Bonnie's in-laws and several of Bob's pallbearer friends joined us there. While I visited with neighbors, who stopped by to see the action, part of the time I also took care of Amy's young girls in Krista's camper on the farmyard. The babies were just too young to be in the filth of the farmhouse.

While I was busy with my tasks, this group of men and women set about tackling the trash-ridden, filthy farmhouse in which Bob had been living. The three oldest grandsons, now six-years-old and old enough to stay safe, were allowed free reign of this "farm world" to explore where Grandpa Bob had lived.

Two large dumpsters, which had been ordered by Bonnie during the week between Bob's death and his funeral, had been delivered and sat the length of the front sidewalk leading up to the house. After some light bulbs were replaced in the otherwise dark house, the true essence of the mess came to light.

Those in the house, armed with shovels and garbage bags, set about shoveling out the contents of the house. While our girls and Bonnie's mother-in-law cleaned out the kitchen cupboards and countertops, the men in the house swept and shoveled the contents of the dining room, living room, and downstairs bedroom. There were mounds of empty tin cans, jars of canned pickles Amy had given him, which he had never eaten, dirty dishes, piles of papers, receipts, and cancelled check blanks, and even the skeletons of a few dead birds. There was just plainly a lot of paper trash, which had never been disposed of. As the multiple bags were filled, Bonnie's father-in-law hauled garbage bag after garbage bag out, gradually filling each dumpster. Likewise, Bonnie's husband and a few others hauled out soiled and moldy furniture, which was all thrown over and skewed throughout the rooms, to those same dumpsters.

I tried to help at first, but soon found myself unable to continue. "I just can't do this," I said, sitting down on one of the two, dusty, film-coated, kitchen chairs. Between my extremely low hemoglobin and the emotional backlash of seeing dishes, which had been mine during our marriage, and other clutter cleaned off of the kitchen countertops and out of the cupboards was more than with which I could deal.

As trash was swept and gathered, the dust and mold in the air became almost unbearable. It was like a heavy fog enveloping the space of the interior rooms. It seemed unbelievable that someone could exist in the conditions of the farmhouse, which definitely had not been cleaned in any way for the twenty years since I had left.

While Krista and Amy joined the women inside, their husbands, along with a few of Bob's friends, began cleaning up the farmyard outside. Bonnie and her husband, Kevin, then joined them to clean up numerous pieces of soiled t-shirts, sweatshirts, and denim jeans, which had been left to rot on the ground between grass, weeds, and sprouting trees. These items were just strewed wherever they had fallen.

Amy's husband, Lars, retrieved the large, new lawn mower Bob had just purchased during the summer from its hiding place in the milk room of the barn. He started it for the first time and was mowing grass and weeds. Meanwhile, son-in-law Lucas and another of Bob's friends were operating chainsaws, cutting young trees, and removing branches, which hung in the way of the working crew. The men started a fire to burn all the debris—old papers, tax documents, mattresses, books—located on a section of the black, plow ground along the driveway of a nearby field.

When darkness fell that evening, most of the family retreated to nearby hotels while Bob's friends scattered to their respective homes. Lars and Lucas remained back at the farmyard to watch the still burning and smoldering fire. They spent the night in the camper.

We knew the day after the funeral would be filled with much the same activity as the upstairs of the house and the basement were still waiting to be emptied. That evening, however, those of us with asthma needed our inhalers to breathe following the afternoon's cleaning chores. Breathing freely once again, we fell into bed. It had been a long, very tiring day.

Morning woke with rain coming down, which added the element of mud to the already existing mess. One of our son-in-law's strewed some straw on the muddy grass going up to the house to help with the slipperiness. The three upstairs bedrooms, the storage room, and the bathroom were emptied of their contents, which then were added to the filling dumpsters—old sheets, pillows, dirty towels, remnants of long-abandoned kids' toys, which had never been claimed.

The basement was rid of those things—mostly wet, dirty clothing and a few old, stainless steel, milking machines, some empty fruit jars, an old minnow bucket—that had to be carried out. An old freezer and refrigerator remained, along with a few other items.

The grandsons explored despite the rain. They went through buildings and back behind the barn collecting items along the way. They also were in the upstairs of the house when the toys were being thrown. The three of them came out each holding a G.I. Joe at one point to take home to their own collections. When wet and cold, they joined me and the granddaughters in the heated camper, which felt soothing compared to the cool, wet weather outside.

While I and my granddaughters were in the camper, we snacked on leftover funeral food—buns with ham, potato chips—while baby

Maggie, Amy's youngest daughter, who was seventeen months old at that time, was tasting the dill pickles.

"Maggie, what did you do with that pickle you just had in your mouth?" I asked.

She pointed to the jar, which was about half full of pickles with their brine.

"You didn't put that pickle back in the jar, did you?" As she nodded, I already knew the answer.

Amanda, her three-year-old sister, just laughed, "She sucked the juice out of it and put it back!" Maggie nodded.

But by that time Maggie was dumping the crushed potato chips left in a bag onto a paper plate and picking ham slices out of an open bun, licking her fingers. As she did so, she noticed her dad, Lars, loading items on his trailer.

"Daddy, daddy," she exclaimed wanting to make her way to the door of the camper.

"No, Maggie. Daddy's working. He can't take you right now. We're going to stay here in the camper where it's warm and dry. We don't want to get all wet from the rain!" I told her.

With that, I started a hide-and-seek game putting a cup down the front of her shirt to hold her attention so all the adults could continue with their work.

By late afternoon, everyone there, including me, made a walk through the house making sure everything that needed to be removed was out of it. The task was complete. The filthy farmhouse, which had been my house with Bob for over twenty years and which I had kept neat and clean, was now a deserted-looking mess. There was no effort to clean any of the flat surfaces of the dirt, hay, straw, and any other debris left on them. A thick layer of sticky dust covered everything. But wiping all those surfaces and sweeping or vacuuming were not worth the time and effort. We were quite sure the house would be demolished anyway. It seemed fitting. The farmhouse, as well as its owner, who was now dead, would be ashes to ashes and dust to dust.

I said what I thought was a final "good-bye" to the house on the farm I had moved to upon Bob's and my marriage forty-three years earlier. A lot of water had gone over the dam since that hopeful wedding day. There was finally finality to that chapter of my life—or was there?

The girls, their husbands and families, and I, each in our own vehicles, headed back to our respective homes, hoping to get there before the impending darkness. I headed back to Minneapolis. Krista and Lucas with their boys headed back, with camper in tow, to their home in Mounds View, Minnesota. Amy and Lars pulled a trailer with Bob's new lawn mower and a four-wheeler bound to be resurrected to their place of residence in Ellsworth, Wisconsin. Bonnie and Kevin headed to the airport for the flight back to their home in Valparaiso, Indiana. The funeral weekend was quite the weekend. But now it was over, and, I think, everyone would agree that leaving the weekend in the rearview mirror was a good thing. Everyone would be back at their respective jobs on Monday. Everyone except me.

CHAPTER 4

Disjointed Time

WITH OUR GIRLS and their families back at their homes and normal lives, I was alone in the Twin Cities the Monday following that busy funeral weekend. I felt like I was not completely present in the slow moments of the day. I spent part of the afternoon simply driving along Minnehaha Parkway both enjoying the nature of it and partly lost in my own thoughts reviewing that through which I had just lived. I felt the same as always, living in the same place, doing familiar tasks and activities. But I was also changed by all that had transpired. Although I had returned to my home, part of my mind was still out at the farm wanting to be sure that all I had just lived through was, indeed, real. A feeling of disorientation flooded over me, much the same feeling I had the weekend and next weeks following Bob's hospitalization and surgeries. In trying to come to terms with the month I had just lived through, in my mind, I reviewed the events from beginning to end.

It was late August when, following his many health complaints, the situation with Bob came to a head. Because, after the bleed he had had out of his eye, nose, and mouth, I insisted he see the doctor or I would call his boss, he did go to the emergency room in Arlington. He gloated upon calling me when he arrived home.

"It's only a sinus infection," he told me in his "wise guy" voice. He continued, "The doctor said that you can bleed like that from too much sinus pressure. I got some antibiotics to take."

I was in disbelief, so I replied, "I don't think so. This has been going on too long. You need to see your regular doctor. You need to have your head checked out with an MRI or a CAT scan! That bleed could happen again, and it could be fatal!"

To my amazement, he listened and made an appointment with his doctor for the soonest he could get in. That would be the Wednesday following Labor Day.

In the meantime, he wanted to ride with me to Amy and Lars' cabin to celebrate their son, Will's, sixth birthday. So that's what we did having no idea what was going on with Bob's head and health.

We drove up to the cabin on the Saturday of Labor Day weekend as did Krista and Lucas and their boys. That night, the children's parents wanted Bob and me to babysit the grandkids so that they could go out to a local bar. Bob agreed that we would babysit the five kids. I was hesitant. With my very low hemoglobin, I had little energy. Also, I knew Bob had no idea what he was agreeing to and would be of little help in the process. Nevertheless, the parents took him up on it very quickly and left for the evening.

While we were taking care of the grandkids, Bob played a game of Battleship with Will. When they were finished, the children were getting wild and boisterous. While I was trying to make order, he seemed to be taking forever to pick up all the Battleship pieces, put them in their container, and put the game away. I was starting to lose my patience when I observed the difficulty that he was having grasping the small pieces with his fingers. I was about to complain to him, but in watching his incapacity in grasping, I fell silent.

Since the kids were not listening to my reprimands, I decided that it was bedtime.

"I'll take Will and Amanda (Amy and Lars' oldest two) upstairs for bed. You take Henry and Hendon (Krista and Lucas' twins) downstairs for bed. Make sure they go to the bathroom before climbing into bed," I commanded.

When the grandkids were settled for the night, Bob laid down on the couch and fell asleep while I straightened up the cabin. Soon their parents arrived home. All was quiet by then.

The next day, I told the parents how wild that the babysitting time had been. Bob was no help with discipline, and I was worn out. I swore to myself that I would not get caught in that kind of babysitting situation with Bob again. I didn't know then that there was a bomb about to go off in our lives, and that that would be the final babysitting situation ever with Bob.

The Sunday of Labor Day weekend went smoothly until evening. We had made tacos for dinner. For some reason, while Lars and Lucas were out on the deck, Bob, who was still eating a taco, had walked down the deck steps and onto the freshly mown lawn in his stocking feet. Amy was dismayed. He would come in with those same stocking feet and drag the freshly cut grass into the cabin.

"Mom, yell out to Dad to get off the grass with his stocking feet," Amy directed me.

Opening the sliding, patio door, I looked at Bob and conveyed the message, "Get off the cut grass with your stocking feet."

He came up the deck steps with an angry face and started yelling at me, "You're always bossing me around!" he shouted as he stepped through the door

At that time Amy said, "She was conveying my message. What, were you, born in a barn?"

"Yes, I was born in a barn," he retorted angrily.

Krista added some comment to that at which time Bob hollered something back. Somehow the shouting match went to the subject of Bob not having helped the girls pay for their college educations, and what a lost cause it was trying to make a go of it on the farm.

I said, referring to my leaving him and the farm, "I could see nothing was ever going to become of it."

"That's because you left!" he replied.

"You made it impossible to stay," I shouted back.

He headed for the couch and covered his head with a blanket. I made it clear that I left him and the farm because he constantly beat me up with his words and his fists.

Lucas and Lars were disturbed that the grandkids had witnessed all of this. And everyone except Bob headed out to have a bonfire. In the meantime, Lars redirected the kids' attention by helping them search for frogs.

The adults discussed the verbal altercation that had just occurred and Bob's outburst. I tried to let all of it flow through and away from me fearing what the drive home with him would be like the next afternoon. Bob stayed on the couch with his head covered with the blanket all night.

The next morning, Sunday, when I got up and came down the stairs from my bedroom, Bob was sitting in the recliner watching the grandchildren play in their pajamas. Lars grilled fish for lunch, we ate, and we headed for home. Not another word was said about the tense blowup the night before.

We talked very little about unimportant topics on the way home. In fact, Bob was extremely quiet, which was certainly not his usual behavior. Often, he would talk practically nonstop. For about forty miles of the trip, he said nothing at all. I did not look towards him during that time. I thought maybe he had fallen asleep. I'll never know if he slept or if his brain issue made him lose track of the miles that we drove. When we were within thirty miles of my home, he asked if we were passing through a town that we had passed a half hour earlier. That made me wonder, but I said nothing.

When we arrived back at my condo, he gathered his belongings from my car and put them in his own car, which he had driven from the farm to my condo before the weekend and which had remained in the condo parking lot throughout the time we were away. He got into his car and left for the farm. We didn't say good-bye to each other. We never did when we met to share a ride to one of our daughters' properties. We would each just go our separate ways—until the next time, which could be weeks or months apart.

I wasn't thinking about the fact that he had his doctor's appointment the following Wednesday, two days after we parted. I was busy working on items for my fall craft sales and cleaning in my condo.

At about four o'clock in the afternoon, he called. "I need a ride to Abbott-Northwestern Hospital. If I get a fellow bus driver to drive me part way, I need you to meet me there. They won't let me drive my car," he said.

I don't know why I agreed, but I did. I guess I didn't think of actually having a choice. I felt he really needed the help. And the need was very immediate by the tone of his voice because a neurologist would be staying at the hospital overtime to meet him when he arrived. So, I headed west out of the Twin Cities and met him and his driver at a McDonald's, a little over half of the way out to the farm.

As he switched cars, the person, who had driven him that far, gave me an envelope to give to the doctors in the emergency ward at the hospital. She simply said, "He's very confused." He seemed not only confused, but completely lost, like he was not quite there. I glanced at the report in the envelope. I surmised, between all the medical terms, that the CAT scan he had had that day indicated there was a large mass in his brain.

The trip back into the Twin Cities was slow because we were heading in during rush hour with plenty of traffic. After about an hour, we reached the hospital where they were expecting him. He was immediately taken to a room.

"Do you want me to come along?" I asked.

A docile man I was not accustomed to nodded.

Once in the room, a doctor came and asked him some questions. Then he was taken for an MRI, which showed similar results to the CAT scan he had had earlier. While he was waiting for that MRI, Bob spoke on the phone to a farmer, who was wanting to get busy with the tiling of one of his fields, which he had arranged to be done that September. Bob told him to hold on with the project because he was in the metro hospital, Abbott-Northwestern, to which I had brought him. Bob also hinted that he wanted someone to come and water a bull, which was being kept in one of the barns.

"I've heard people arranging for the care of dogs and cats or even a bird," the attending nurse laughed, "but never a pet bull."

After some time, as other tests were being run, Bob noticed how tired I was. "You should go home. You look very tired. They're keeping me in the hospital overnight. Could you pick up a pair of glasses on the way back tomorrow?"

He was very civil. He was unusually thoughtful. I left, driving the seven miles in city traffic back to my condo.

The next day I didn't hurry back to the hospital. After all, I was not his wife, so I felt there would be no expectation of my being there early. I'd done what he'd ask me to do by delivering him to the hospital. I figured he would call if he needed me to return to the hospital to pick him up if they were discharging him earlier than I planned to return. In the hurry to get there the night before, he had forgotten his reading glasses in his car parked back in Arlington. Late in the afternoon, I headed back to the hospital, picking up a pair of reading glasses at Walgreen's on the way.

When I got to his room at the hospital, he was lying on his back in bed. He said he had had a test. The doctors were hoping he would have blockage in an artery so they could "shut off" some of the "feeding" of what had been determined to be a vascular tumor of the cerebellum. He was proud that there was no blockage. But that did not turn out to be a good thing. They could do nothing to keep the tumor from growing nor could they use that blockage to reduce bleeding during surgery.

Bob said to me when I arrived, "I thought you'd come sooner. I was anxious," indicating he was nervous about having the procedure before it was done. I did not respond. I was not his wife. I did not have the responsibility of soothing his fear. He had never accompanied me to the doctor when I was going through a scary procedure. Especially scary was a breast lump I had found when Amy was three. He did not accompany me to the doctor, to the mammogram, or to find out the results two weeks later. Instead he complained about the time it was taking and how much it was going to cost. I had to go through the whole scary process myself. But I kept quiet at this time figuring it was not going to help to pick a fight with a man, who had just found out that he had a brain tumor.

Instead, I made conversation with the nurse about her shoes as she helped Bob get ready to return with me to my condo. They were allowing him to leave for the night as long as he stayed in the Twin Cities. There was the possibility he would develop a bleed in his groin where they had gone in with the probe to check for any artery blockage. They wanted him close to the hospital just in case. They also gave specific instructions. He was to be back the following week on Friday morning for the first of two surgeries—to place a tube in his skull to drain off hydrocephalic fluid, which had developed around his skull and neck. The tumor would be removed the Monday following the tube surgery. In between his return home and his coming back, he was not to drive or go anywhere as a stroke or seizure could be very likely.

I suppose we had some dinner upon arriving home although I don't remember. He slept on my couch. The next day, I drove him back out to Arlington to pick up his car telling him specifically the directions he had been given. "You are to pick up groceries for the week, then you are to return home and stay there until next Thursday when I pick you up for your surgeries. I'll be at the farm at two o'clock, so be ready."

Then he drove off to supposedly do as he was told. And I headed back to the Twin Cities.

I later learned that he did everything except stay at home for that week. Even though he could have had a stroke or seizure at any moment, he was out driving. He drove to the bus garage and spoke to his boss. He drove to a nearby town to pick up ground corn for his pet bull and fill his pickup with gas. At the gas station he lost his temper because they would not accept his check as payment and his debit card would not work. He then drove to the bank some fifteen miles away, angry that someone at the bank would not bring him cash to pay his gas bill. At that time, he exhibited very intense anger.

"I'd never seen him that angry!" the friend, who was with him, recalled later.

The instance of anger at Amy's cabin on Labor Day weekend coupled with the intense anger he showed on this day, I think, showed his loss of emotional control due to the tumor. Although I knew he could lose his temper quite easily, the tumor was affecting his reasoning and self-control even more.

The next Thursday, the second full week in September, I was at the farm to pick him up at promptly two o'clock p.m. I wanted to pick him up and get back into the Twin Cities before we would get hung up in rush hour traffic. I knew it would be practically impossible to pick him up on Friday morning and get him to the hospital by eight o'clock in the morning. So, I had chosen instead to pick him up the afternoon before and let him sleep on my couch another night so we could meet the timeline set by the doctor.

When I arrived, Bob was sitting in his car looking at some papers rather than waiting for me in the house. I shuddered when I saw the condition of the farm. It was overgrown with tall grass, weeds, brush, and young trees. It definitely didn't look like the farm I had left over twenty years earlier. I knew things had gone downhill, but I didn't realize just how badly everything had changed. I could barely see the house through the trees. What was once our large, open farmyard was grown in with trees, brush, weeds, and tall grass.

He walked over to my car with a loose bundle of clothing in his arm and some loose papers, which would turn out to be his will and health care directive. The papers were all crinkled, disorganized, and water damaged. He brought a package of new check blanks, and a greeting card with a business card in it. That card had been sent to him by the new pastor of his church, whom he had never met. He threw these things into the back seat of my car. He then paused for a moment, making a slow, full circle with his body scanning the farmyard. He climbed into the car saying, "In case I never see all this again." With that, he climbed into the car. I backed the car towards the barn turning around, and we were off.

As we neared the end of the farm's driveway, I was about to turn north to head back into the Twin Cities when he stopped me. "Right! Right! We have to turn right! We have to go to the post office! We have to forward my mail!" I had forgotten we had this task to do. So, I changed direction, turned right, and we headed into town to the post office.

Once there, the postal clerk asked, as she was filling out the mail forwarding form, "How long do you want the forwarding to be in effect?"

We looked at each other. We were both thinking at the same time that we had no idea. Even if Bob survived the surgeries, he would likely have to be in rehabilitation for a while. Just how long that "while" would be, we had no idea.

Finally, I said, "Six months."

It was a guess, but I thought it would at least buy time.

With that task completed, I felt pressured to leave town quickly. I was seeing people I knew from when I had lived there. I felt uncomfortable being seen with Bob. Gossip spreads quickly in small towns, and I did not want to be the subject of it. What would people think if I were seen driving Bob around town? I headed to the street, which would take us up to the highway leading to the Twin Cities. We headed out of town to the northeast without any further delays.

On Thursday evening, Bob was sitting in my recliner while I made dinner. Strangely, he commented that the cooking dinner "smelled good."

Later, as we were eating, he complimented me on the chicken. "This chicken is really good!"

I was surprised. He had always heartily eaten what I had cooked, but he had never complimented me on any of it.

"It's a rotisserie chicken from Walmart," I responded.

I had merely warmed up a rotisserie chicken I had picked up at Walmart the day before. I am left to wonder why I was receiving compliments that evening. Was he trying to say something he had on his mind? Was he feeling this might be his last homemade meal? Was he trying to show appreciation? In some way, was he trying to say he was sorry for the behavior he had displayed to me and the ways he had hurt me physically and mentally while we were married? I will never know.

The next morning, he was showering early while I also was getting ready for the trip to the hospital. We arrived at the hospital early, and he was taken into a surgery waiting room to get ready. When he was ready for the surgery, I was called into the room. As well, the anesthesiologist, the surgeon, and the surgeon's nurse practitioner were in the room.

"What would you like to get out of the surgery?" the surgeon asked.

I thought it a rather strange question, but Bob answered, "I'd like to see my grandsons grow up." For the first time he had tears in his eyes.

As Bob said this, I felt angry. It touched an old hurt for me. Bob had wanted a son. When our third daughter was born, who was to be our last child, Bob had been disappointed. He had left the hospital and did not come back that evening. Now he was mentioning his "grandsons" while excluding his granddaughters, I thought. Then, I realized that it was probably just his limited way of saying he wanted to see his all of his grandchildren grow up. He was never very good at verbalizing his thoughts. This was not the time to correct him or give him grief.

The nurse said, "Kisses and hugs before surgery."

I did not offer any. I was not his wife. I did not feel the desire or the need to do so. I left the surgery preparation room and went to wait in the family waiting area. With that, he was wheeled into surgery.

I did wait for him at the hospital that very long day. I had brought my embroidery project. I worked on that as the hours ticked by. I broke up the day around two in the afternoon by going over to the little, lunch café at the hospital.

Around five p.m., the surgeon came to meet me. "He's out of surgery. All went well. He's in recovery. They will come and get you when he's ready."

I then waited another five hours before they called me in to his area in recovery. He was alert and speaking to the recovery nurse. There was a plastic tube coming out of the top of the right side of his forehead, which was bound in place with a tube of netting.

The nurse said, "He's been awake for some time, but we were waiting for a room in ICU to become available for him." We spoke briefly.

Bob commented, "You looked very tired. You should go home."

So, I did.

The next day, Bonnie flew in. She and I went to see Bob later in the afternoon. He was sitting up in a chair in his room and watching football. He said Krista had been there earlier. But there was only a brief conversation overall. He said nothing the girls might want to know considering the seriousness of the next surgery that was to be on the following Monday.

On Sunday, I did not go back to the hospital. Since my hemoglobin was still really low, I was beside myself with tiredness. (I was in the process of being treated for low hemoglobin at that time). Bob texted me at one point asking if I was at the hospital having a blood transfusion. He wanted to come to the infusion lab to see me. The nurses, however, would not allow it, saying he could have a stroke or seizure by moving.

I responded, "No. I'm at home resting."

I had chosen to remain at home to rest. I did not feel the need to see him again. After all, I was not his wife.

Our girls saw him for a visit one last time that Sunday before the actual surgery to remove the tumor. They expressed disappointment that he really had nothing of substance to say to them considering he was facing "life and death" surgery and might never get to speak with them again. He might have told them that he loved them. He might have told them that he was proud of them (They all have degrees and are accomplished professionals. They have beautiful families). He did not. He always had had very little ability to think of others over himself. Plus, as I have said before, he had difficulty expressing his thoughts. Either way, this was their last communication with him. And he failed, or was unable, to say what they needed to hear.

On the Monday of the third week in September, the Monday of Bob's surgery to remove the tumor, I did not go to the hospital to be there before he went into surgery. He was going in very early. Also, I had an afternoon appointment for another matter to which I planned to go.

Our girls were meeting at the hospital in the afternoon. I was meeting them there to be present when Bob came out of surgery. Around six o'clock in the evening the surgeon came to the waiting area.

"He's come successfully out of surgery," the surgeon relayed to us. "He's in recovery. The nurse will come to get you when he's ready."

When Bonnie heard that, she left to catch a flight back home to Indiana in order to be at work the next morning. Krista headed home to take care of her boys. Amy waited with me.

Around eight p.m., Amy and I were allowed to see Bob in his ICU room. He was still very incoherent as they were settling him into his hospital bed. His tongue, which looked very huge and swollen, was hanging out of his mouth.

"Pull your tongue into your mouth," the nurse commanded.

If there was any movement of the tongue, it was very slight.

Again, the attending nurse commanded, "Pull your tongue back into your mouth."

Bob did hear the command because he did pull it in a little bit. But he wasn't able to pull it in completely.

I think the nurse felt we were disturbed by what we were seeing because, at that time, she sent us back into a waiting area while several medical people were serving his needs. As we left the room, the surgeon and his nurse practitioner notified us that there would be a check in with them at nine o'clock the next morning, Tuesday.

Amy and I waited and waited. With my low hemoglobin, I was beside myself with tiredness. Finally, around eleven thirty, the attending nurse came out to get us.

Noticing I was sitting with my head lying on my purse on the arm rest of my chair, the nurse said, "You are tired." She paused and added, " You may go in now."

Bob was then settled in the room with monitors hooked up everywhere. His tongue was in his closed mouth. And he was asleep. At that time, we each left for our respective homes.

I remember nothing after my head hit the pillow. It had been a long, stressful day.

On Tuesday morning, Krista and I were at the hospital for the doctor's check-in at nine. He and his nurse reported that vital signs were good. So far, he was doing well. The orderlies then took Bob for a CAT scan. I waited in Bob's room. Krista went to work.

As Bob was taken out, the nurse practitioner said to me, "He will have a long rehabilitation."

I responded, "He can't live with any of us."

That may seem mean, but Bob had burned his bridges. He had been cruel, abusive, uncaring, and unsupportive. We had all made our lives without him except for very brief events. We could not be nursemaids to him now. We just could not do that.

The surgeon's nurse practitioner also mentioned that there was a genetic component to Bob's tumor. She suggested that maybe we, as his family, would want to do some genetic counseling about it. I did not take her comments too seriously at the time. I think I was just so absorbed in the ongoing events that I was not able to go to that place to even ask a question. I did not understand what she meant by "genetic component." She went on with her work. And I focused on what was happening immediately in front of me.

When Bob was returned to his room following the scan, he was awake. I was telling the attending nurse how I had had to force him to go to the doctor because he would not quit driving bus.

"I was afraid he would take down a whole busload of kids with him!" I said.

At that, Bob, who was now awake, got my attention by making a sign to me. He circled his bandaged head with his arm and made what looked like a "talking" sign with his thumb and fingers. Then he repeated his motions, again circling his head and making the talking motion.

I looked at him and said, "I know, my talking is hurting your head," and I turned around and left the room.

I didn't go back to the hospital that day. At home, however, I called one of Bob's sisters and told her what was going on. It was still hopeful at this point. By evening, though, he was not breathing well on his own and had to be intubated.

The next morning, Wednesday, the third week in September, the surgeon's nurse practitioner called me early. She said that they wanted to do another CAT scan following the one they had done the night before. They had noticed the night before that there was a slight bleed in the space of Bob's cerebellum near where the tumor was removed. They wanted to make sure that it had not grown bigger and was not a stroke.

I did not go into the hospital that day during the daytime. I was getting reports that Bob was not awake. Instead, I called the pastor, whose business card Bob had left with me. She agreed to visit him on Friday at noon.

In the evening I felt I needed to go see him to see if he would respond in some way to my voice, even by squeezing my hand. I took his warm hand.

"Bob. Bob," I said softly.

Then I spoke a little louder. "Bob," and again, "Bob."

There was no response. He did not move in any way.

That evening, as I pulled out of the hospital parking lot, I had a sinking feeling.

On Thursday of that week, I received reports from the hospital that there was no change in Bob. My agitation built throughout the day as it became clear to me at this point that Bob's recovery was not going in the right direction. I was starting to go through the sequence of events over the last two-and-one-half weeks in my mind. Things were looking dim, even for me, who did not feel emotional connection to him anymore. But I had somehow become "connected" by simply helping him when he needed my help. I was feeling that what we were looking at was his death.

The next morning, Friday, the surgeon's nurse practitioner evidently tried to call early. But I had not slept well during the night, so by morning I was sleeping soundly. I did not hear the phone ring. Not getting me on the phone, she called Bonnie, who was actually his healthcare guardian. It was good that she got the call, although it turned out to be very upsetting for her.

Bob was no longer responding. His eyes were blank. The decision had to be made to either let him go or do surgery to remove what had become a clot in the space left by the removal of the tumor. Such a surgery would likely leave him alive but possibly in a vegetative state. But, even by taking him off the ventilator, there was a slim chance that he might live and also be in a vegetative state. We all knew the answer that had to be given. He had clearly stated in his healthcare directive that he did not want any unusual means to keep him alive if there was no possibility of him having a full, "normal" life.

When Bonnie received the call, she knew the answer. She was just walking into work at her job in Indiana when she answered the call, so walked into her office and broke down crying. Even in a situation where most of the ties of love have been severed, that is a difficult call for anyone to make. She needed the cry to release the emotion. She was very brave. And since she was in Indiana and we were in the hospital in Minnesota, we could not be there to support her.

Upon hearing of Bob's condition and knowing that removal of the breathing tube would most likely lead to his death, I phoned his sister.

She asked, "Can you keep him alive until tomorrow?"

I responded, "No, we will be removing the tube this afternoon." I was not trying to be mean. I did not want Bob lying there suffering an extra day. I hope she understood that.

The pastor went in on Friday morning to pray for Bob before I was able to call her about his impending possible death. I phoned her around eleven o'clock and told her the news. She had been early and had already prayed with him when she received my call. She was still at the hospital, so she asked if my family and I could meet her there. I shared the news with Amy and Krista, who called their husbands. We then met at the hospital around one o'clock that afternoon.

Krista and Lucas, Amy and Lars, and I met with the pastor as we all prayed The Lord's Prayer at Bob's bedside. Bob had hurt all of us badly. He had done and said things that were unimaginable to those he was supposedly "loving." This, however, was a difficult moment for all of us. I am glad the pastor was there to strengthen us. As she left, I agreed to call her later that evening to update her.

Around two p.m., the hospital personnel removed the breathing tube and started palliative care. We, as a family, went to a conference room for a few hours to wait. The nurse practitioner came in and asked if we had any questions. Since we had none to ask, she went back out to the nurse's station and about her business. Krista and Lucas left at that time to be home for their boys after school.

At some point, later in the afternoon, Amy and Lars and I went back to Bob's room to wait. Bob's breathing was very labored, and his blood pressure was rising quickly. His body was straining to stay alive.

Around six o'clock in the evening, with progress seeming very slow, I decided to go home to pick up the paperwork Bob had left with me. Lars, an attorney, would need it going forward. I was half-way back to the hospital when I got the text from Amy.

Amy asked, "Are you going to be back soon, Mom?"

Since I was driving, I couldn't respond.

It took me awhile to get back to Bob's room. Because of the possibility of an impending thunderstorm, I decided to park my car in the hospital's parking ramp instead of in the open lot. The ramp was at the other end of the hospital block, so I had to walk the entire length of the hospital to get to his ICU. With my low hemoglobin, I had to stop at times to catch my breath.

When I returned to Bob's room, Amy was sitting on a chair, and Lars was holding an ice pack over Bob's eyes since we had agreed to donate his corneas. Bob had passed at eight minutes past seven p.m. Lars asked if I would hold the ice so he could attend to another matter. As I held it, I gradually slid it up to Bob's forehead. His eyes were nearly closed, but through the remaining slits I could see they were completely vacant. All life was gone out of them.

After staying in Bob's room for what seemed a long time, we gave the hospital staff the name of the mortuary we would be using, Kolden Funeral Home in Arlington, Minnesota. Then I answered the questions necessary to get the directive for the cornea transplant in motion. At that, we left the Bob's room and the hospital.

The surgeon, who had performed Bob's surgeries, was near the nurses' desk. Upon hearing of Bob's death, he was deeply upset. He sat down on a nurses' stool as he processed it. Then he said that there most likely had been very minute tumors, too small to see on an MRI and the CAT scans, going down his brain stem. Bleeding from one of these developing tumors was likely the cause of the bleed in Bob's brain. He also told us that, over time, these tumors would have likely grown, fed by the blood in Bob's arteries. The rest of Bob's life would have been the cycle of removing tumors and the resulting rehabilitation.

When I got home that Friday night, the evening of Bob's death, it was nearly midnight. I met another woman in my condo building, also a pastor, as I was coming up from the parking garage beneath the building.

She asked, "How is your ex-husband?"

I answered, "He died tonight."

I can remember feeling how little expression there was in my voice. The death was not like losing a loved one. I felt separated from the death in a strange way. There were no tears.

Upon returning to my condo, I first called Bob's pastor as I had said I would. It was late, and I knew she was probably staying up to receive the call. Then I received a call from the eye bank to complete the paperwork for the cornea donations.

It was nearly two a.m. when I finally crept into bed. It was then that I processed the depth of what the surgeon had explained. If Bob had not died following the removal of this tumor, there would have been another, and then, another. The rest of his life would have very likely been in a rehabilitation facility. Life as he had known it, would have been gone. I realized, as I laid there, that perhaps his death, even though I had not even entertained the idea that this might be the result, was a blessing. That gave me strength to face the following week.

On the Saturday morning following Bob's death, the sun rose bright and sunny. I was awakened by a call from the mortuary in Arlington.

The mortuary assistant informed me, "I am just leaving to come up to Abbott Hospital to pick up Bob's body."

"Thanks for your call," I responded.

Then I laid back down on the bed trying to process all of the events of the last week. I felt like I had been in a whirlwind and had now been plunked down back to earth. I was just starting to grasp the reality of the situation.

The last Sunday of September was a quiet day of rest, a rest I so badly needed. Again, it was a beautiful, bright, sunny day. It would have been a wonderful day to spend in a park having a picnic lunch or being out on the open water taking in the warm breeze. I am not sure I even went out that day. I merely watched from inside my condo like I was looking at a television screen outside my bedroom window.

Monday was cloudy and humid. In the morning, I searched through one of the top drawers of my china cupboard looking for the old Arlington phone book I had saved from when I had first left the farm. 1994-1995 it said. Searching through the numbers and searching websites, I tried to find someone, who would pick up the pet bull that I knew Bob had kept in the shed behind the barn. I didn't know if the shipping person, who had hauled cattle for us when I was still on the farm twenty years earlier, continued to do so. Luckily, I got through to him and explained the situation. We had a pleasant conversation. After all, I had known him for twenty-some years before I'd left the farm. He seemed to indicate that everyone in Arlington had already heard the news of Bob's death. Some things about small towns never change, I thought.

After that, I called the lumberyard in town. I wanted locks put on Bob's farmhouse doors. I knew it had been sitting open for over a week. I knew that there really wasn't anything of any value in the house. But now that the news was out that Bob had died, anyone could prowl through the house and, perhaps, even hurt themselves.

My next call was to the church's cemetery association. I made arrangements for Bob's cemetery plot. I was able to get the one that Bob had indicated that he wanted. He had said, if he did not survive, he wanted to be next to his cousin, Bernie, and wanted to be facing his farm so he could "see it."

I had a therapy appointment in the afternoon after which I was scheduled to pick up Bonnie at the airport. She would stay through early Wednesday morning to help the other two girls with funeral planning and taking care of other details. After picking her up, she and I headed to a restaurant the girls had chosen in Woodbury to meet Krista and Amy to form the plan of attack for the next day. The girls had one day to get everything arranged, get the information they would need, and plan for the coming funeral and cleaning up the estate.

Tuesday of that last week in September was a marathon day. The first stop was the lumberyard for payment of the locks they had placed on the house. Second was a check in at the motel where Amy and Lars and family would be staying on the weekend. Third was a stop at the school to find out how to access the retirement account, which Bob had through the school from his bus driving years. Fourth was a stop at the bank to find out about Bob's accounts

The fifth stop was the long one at the mortuary. Bob's clothes had been washed and ironed along with his shoes, socks, and belt and packed in plastic bag. I knew the mortician would want them that day. There was much paperwork to be completed also. Then we were shown into the casket room. Bob specifically wanted a casket funeral rather than cremation. We were going to honor that desire. The girls picked a simple, wooden casket and an appropriate vault. Together we chose the memorial and thank you cards, picking a verse about farming for inside the memorial folder.

By the time all those details had been decided, the sun was mid-way down in the west, and we still had two more stops in town. We split up to take care of those two things. Bonnie and Amy went to the accountant to get information about Bob's retirement accounts. Krista and I went to the florist. We made simple choices there because Bob was not a fan of flowers. We chose a bouquet of fall grasses, leaves, cattails, with a few mums. On the casket would be three red roses from the girls. Both the arrangement and the roses would have burlap bows. When asked what wording to put on the ribbon "Father" or "Dad", it was an easy choice. He was a "father" but not a "dad." I think most people will understand the difference.

The second to last stop would be the church. I had written out the funeral service order, Bible verses, and hymns for the funeral. I left that paper on the pastor's desk.

The girls and I then headed out to the farm. At the farm, Bonnie collected any papers she could find that would be useful. She looked for the titles for the vehicles, but she found none. Krista collected a few of her personal items, which had remained up in her bedroom in the farmhouse after she moved out. All three looked around the house and the farmyard, studying its condition. A curious bull was looking out over his fence to see who was stirring in his world. Bonnie moved Bob's vehicles. His car was backed away from the house. The pickup was parked between some of the trees.

We headed back to the Twin Cities as the sun was setting in the west. We ate dinner at a restaurant in Eden Prairie. From my place, everyone, except Bonnie, went their separate ways back home to their families. Bonnie slept the night at my condo. By the time I woke up the next morning, she was already gone to the airport and on her way back to Indiana.

On Wednesday, I wrote the funeral sermon. I didn't struggle with it at all like I sometimes struggled with just what to say in a funeral sermon. I needed to talk about death, the events of the past month, Bob's condition, forgiveness, redemption, and salvation. Bob had gone quickly from driving school bus to being dead. People would want to know how and why. I was the one who knew the details people would want to hear. As a pastor, for me it seemed to be a natural task. In the afternoon I had a doctor's appointment for myself.

On Thursday I had a blood draw to check my hemoglobin. My hemoglobin level was so low, I was scheduled for a blood transfusion at Abbot-Northwestern Hospital later that afternoon. Because the hospital was having trouble matching and cross typing my blood, it was midnight by the time they found blood for me and began the blood transfusion. In the meantime, I was feeling rather emotional being in the hospital where Bob had died so soon after his death. This was really the only sadness I had felt because of his death up to this time.

The blood transfusion was finally finished at four o'clock in the morning. Rather than stay at the hospital until morning, however, I decided to drive home so I could sleep in once I crawled into bed. On the way home, a fox crossed the city street ahead in my headlights. I guess even when the city calms and gets quiet for the night, the wild animals prowl.

Friday was a quiet, restful day. For the first time in a month, I really had the chance to stop and enjoy the solitude. I chose and prepared what I would wear for the funeral. As I said earlier, I thought of wearing my clergy collar, but decided against it since I was not presiding, merely preaching. So, I chose to wear my black pants and suit jacket, which had often been my funeral "outfit." I packed clothes to wear for the clean up at the farm following the funeral—jeans, an old t-shirt, and my old, brown, everyday shoes. I practiced my sermon. Then I did nothing. My mind had been very busy for more days than I could count! Now, finally, because of the blood transfusion, I had energy for myself.

Then came the Saturday of the funeral and the farm cleanup weekend.

Although at the time everything seemed slow, like I was plodding through it, in reality it was a whirlwind. The entire last month had been a whirlwind. I had been sucked up in it, and now, I had been thrown out on the other side. In one month, this living breathing person to whom I had once been married, the father of my children, the grandfather to our grandchildren, who had been very much alive at the beginning of the month, was now gone. I had landed. And I had landed hard, very hard. [APPENDIX V]

CHAPTER 5

An Empty Chair in the Aisle

DURING THE TWO weeks following the funeral, I sorted through sympathy cards and separated out memorial envelopes to form a list of whom to send thank you cards. I searched the internet for address-es that were not on memorials or in the visitation and funeral book. I looked in my old, 1994 Arlington phone book. Satisfied that I had found almost all of the addresses I needed, I set about writing those notes so I could get them in the mail. After five hours, the thank you notes were ready to send. I put the tub of sympathy cards, the funeral book, left over memorial cards, and pictures, which had been saved in a dish tub from the farmhouse cleaning, on the bottom shelf of my coffee table, where it would sit for the next five months, forgotten.

Throughout the whole time, I still felt disbelief that everything in the month of September had transpired. The sense of unreality was consuming. My restlessness, at last, compelled me to make the sixty-mile trip back out to the farm on the second Saturday of October. I had to make it in order to put everything, which had happened, to rest in my mind.

That Saturday had started out sunny and cool. As I travelled south-westward, clouds overtook the sun. As I turned into the farm's drive-way, there were occasional raindrops in the air.

There was much motion on the farmyard. An acquaintance of Bob had paid a lump sum to the estate for the bulk of what was left of Bob's farm machinery. Included in the sale was Bob's 2006 Chevrolet HHR, and various farm tools, his large, Ford tractor, and a few smaller ones, his four-by-four pickup, and his skid steer loader. Members of that family were busy sorting old tires from metal and iron and loading the tires on a hayrack to be disposed of. The large machine shed had been scraped clean of all the hay and straw that had been strewed on the dirt floor over several years. All of that debris was on a pile about ten feet high and thirty feet long waiting to be burned. One man was running the skid steer loader. Another was cutting up old machinery for scrap iron in order to sell it. All of Bob's old cars and trucks, rusted and dilapidated with broken out windows, were strung in a line like a train across the cement that had been the feedlot for the cattle behind the barn. All the manure that had been covering that cement platform had been cleared away. The large, filled, trash containers, which had been left in front of the house two weeks before, had been cleared. Brush and young trees had been removed, and the entire farmyard was clean and open.

I was greeted by one of Bob's friends, who recognized my car, and who was related to the family cleaning up the yard.

"Hi. How are you doing?" was his greeting.

"Good," I responded. "I just had to see how things were going out here."

"We've been very busy you can see," he replied.

"Wow! There's a big change. You've been really busy!" I responded.

At that, he introduced me to his cousin, the buyer, another cousin, and his uncle.

"Hi. Nice to meet you," the uncle greeted me. He showed me the old elevator, which was being broken down to be junked or sold. He told me a little about his wife, who had just passed away in August, and a little about his interactions with Bob.

With that, Bob's friend and his friend's cousin walked with me around the farmyard, now so open that I could see entirely across it. They had to show me how a large tree behind the granary had grown up with a tire around it. Evidently that tire had rested in that spot for a very long time, perhaps over twenty years judging by the size of the tree.

I looked out over the calf yard, now without the fence I had erected with my father-in-law's help in 1975. It was now just smooth grass from one end to the other. I viewed the windbreak Bob and I had planted and so tenderly nursed in 1989. Now full grown, it stood twenty to thirty feet tall. But as I looked out at it, I still saw the rows of baby trees, remembered cutting grass between those trees to keep the weeds down, and how I use to walk through the trees when they were merely five or six feet tall—when it felt like I was walking through a soothing park. Tears came to my eyes. There were so many memories here that I could see now that the overgrowth had been removed.

The cousin put his arm around my shoulder. "Memories. There are so many memories," was all he said.

I know Bob was much different when around these friends than he had been when I was married to him. I had seen the full steam of his anger on many, many occasions. He had put his anger in a compartment by the time he interacted with them. Or, perhaps in some way over time, he had become more docile.

I walked along the vehicles behind the barn, remembering when they were obtained. There was the red, 4 X 4 Chevrolet pickup we had bought used in 1982, tired of getting stuck in the mud on the farmyard. There was the 1984 Cavalier I purchased in 1987 so that we would have a car safe enough to see my mother in the hospital in Mankato. There was the 1992 Silverado pickup, the only vehicle we had ever purchased new. We needed that both to replace the red pickup and to provide another means of transportation when the girls were beginning to drive. Then there was the Old's Calais that Bonnie had purchased while in college and which Bob had refused to let her trade when she bought something newer. Those vehicles had all been part of our family at some point, and they still told of the story of our past.

There were two other vehicles. There was the blue Corsica he had bought to replace the Cavalier after I had left. Finally, there was an old Ford Frontier pickup. When I and the girls had been out to the farm the Tuesday after Bob's death and looking for the vehicle titles, I had suggested they check in the glove compartment of that pickup. As Amy sat on its dusty seat, she opened the glove compartment door. Out fell shredded paper and baby mice. She let out a shriek. Needless to say, that was the only glove compartment checked out that day. The girls would end up getting the titles for the vehicles from the License Division of the State of Minnesota.

I walked through the large, steel, machine shed that we had built in 1990. It had been Bob's longtime dream to have a large, machine shed so that the machinery wouldn't have to stay out in the weather and rust. I remembered that, as badly as Bob wanted it, he never really put the machinery in it once he had it. It did, however, store hay and straw bales, the tractors, seed bags when purchased in the springtime, and occasionally a gravity box with a load of grain in it, which was waiting to be unloaded. I remembered mowing the lawn around all the farm buildings and the machinery left sitting on the lawn. I remembered how difficult and time-consuming it was. I remembered how I often wished Bob would help, and all the hours it took away from my life.

I ended by walking through the dairy barn, which we had remodeled and expanded in 1979. The stainless-steel sinks and milking equipment in the milk room still hung in their respective locations. I thought about whether or not I would still know how to set up the milking claws and run the pipeline washer after all these years. The old, huge, electric motor, which had run the entire milking system, and which Bob had not used since selling the milking cattle in 2002, stood in the corner, covered in dust and cobwebs. The eight-hundred-gallon, stainless steel bulk tank, which, at the time it was purchased, had cost us as much as a new car, had been sold. The large area in the center of the room was empty.

Then, I went through the door into the milking barn itself. Now dry and empty, the walls still wore some of the whitewash from the milking years. The feeding cribs, the stalls, and the gutters had never been cleaned after the cows were shipped. Their contents were completely dried out and turned to dust. The stainless-steel pipeline that circled the entire barn near the ceiling hung heavy with dust and cobwebs. The pen in the northwest corner of the barn was abandoned. The large fans, which were placed above where the cattle had stood in their stalls, which whirled with a loud roar on hot days, were spooky quiet. Only the cooing of a few pigeons in the haybarn sounded within the space.

In the middle of the aisle about midway through the barn was a dark green, comfortably-stuffed, living room recliner of unknown origin. The footrest was up in the reclining position as if someone had just been sitting in it and had climbed out without collapsing it. It struck me that it looked as if its owner had been plucked up and out of it never to return. Perhaps it was a symbol of the reality of the entire situation. I took a deep breath, and I walked out of the barn the same way I had come.

Since the men were all busy working, I simply waved good-bye, turned the car around, and drove down the driveway turning north and then west. It was raining steadily by this time, but I did want to visit the gravesite during this trip as well.

I turned into the cemetery driveway, parking on the slippery grass. I walked over to the unmarked gravesite recognizing it by the freshly turned earth. As I came upon it, I noticed that grass seed had been scattered on the black dirt. It was already sprouting its little spindles—fresh, green grass scattered in a mosaic pattern on the black canvas. At the digging line of the head end, lay the bouquet of the three, red roses and the burlap ribbon with the golden word "Father" still glued to it. Strangely, the three, red roses were not dried up as I would have expected. They were still soft and unusually red. I remember thinking that must have been because of the cool, October air and intermittent rain. I spent a few solemn moments. Then, with my jacket quite soaked, I walked back to the car. Taking off my wet jacket, I climbed into the car, started it, and backed out onto the gravel road once again. The rain stayed with me the entire trip back into the Twin Cities.

At least now, in some way, I was able to find closure. I was able to put everything that had occurred during September—the illness, the hospital, the surgeries, the funeral, and cleaning up the farmhouse and yard—into better perspective. I was able to take some steps forward into the changed reality.

CHAPTER 6

It's Complicated

ANY MARRIAGE THAT ends in divorce is complicated. So many factors, sometimes small and sometimes very great, go into the very difficult decision to divorce. Often there is a lot of hurt by one or both parties, which leads to the very difficult decision to divorce. Shared property and the division of it can be a major issue. Even more major can be the sharing of children. Many horrendous custody battles can often ensue when a couple decides to divorce. Moving, changing jobs, redefining friendships, and issues regarding in-laws and other relatives are just some of the factors that rise to the forefront when a divorce is sought. There has to be a redefinition of self when one is no longer part of the original coupling. In the same way that a divorce can be freeing, it can also end up without completely severing ties with the former spouse, which continue to raise problems. Those who have sailed through a divorce without any of these issues can consider themselves fortunate.

I do not pretend to know all the aspects of divorce that need to be addressed when a couple separates. I am sure I am not evening thinking of some of the difficulties of divorce others have experienced. Although, as a pastor, I have walked with people, who have gone through divorce, I am not an expert. What I share here are the reasons I sought a divorce and my processing having gone through it. What I remember most is that the entire process and the "uncoupling" was not easy by any stretch of the imagination.

Our marriage was one in which abuse was a common element. I experienced, on an on-going and increasing basis, verbal, emotional, and sexual abuse. That was coupled with physical abuse in all forms. I left for my physical safety and to survive emotionally. I left so the girls would not have to live with the on-going verbal and emotional abuse, and what seemed to be more often, the threat of physical abuse. The complete details of my abusive marriage to Bob are detailed in my book, **Butterfly Song** (Plainview Press, 2007). But I will describe it in an abbreviated way here.

In July of 1974, my family and I were busy putting on finishing touches for a day I had looked forward to for many years. The day came, hot and humid as July can be. Bob and I were married in the small, country church where I had grown up. Was I entering marriage with any idea of the on-going abuse, which would define our marriage of almost twenty-four years?

Looking back on it now, I suppose I could have.

Bob and I knew each other throughout our twelve years of elementary and secondary education at the same public school. We had dated since prom of our junior year in high school. We had continued to date through four years of college. We had just graduated with our Bachelor of Arts degrees from the University we had attended.

During that time, physical abuse had occurred on two occasions. The first time was in our fourth year of dating. He had accused me of being jealous of another girl, who lived on our dormitory floor. He had punched me repeatedly in the stomach, knocking me down onto my bed. Afterwards, he looked very confused, like he did not know what had just happened. He took me to the doctor because of an extreme pain in the area of my diaphragm. The next day, when I came back from class, I found a bouquet of flowers in my dormitory room from him.

The second time was in our senior year of college. We had now been dating for five years and wedding plans were in progress to occur after graduation. Bob wanted me to go to the bar with him and some other friends in the evening. I was student teaching at the time. I had full, long days, and would have to be up early the next morning. I was tired, so I refused. He grabbed me by the hand, grasping it hard, and breaking the little finger on my right hand. That time, he blamed me. It was my fault since I had refused to go to the bar with him.

One would think that I should have known better, should have recognized his behaviors as part of the pattern of abuse, and not married him. Yet, in the early 1970's, there was no information available regarding what to look for in an abusive relationship—the abuse, the flowers or other apology, the contriteness, and improved behavior—until the next time! I had never observed an abusive relationship. We had had many good times together. I guess I felt the pressure of college life was affecting him on those few occasions.

My marriage was not the happy, Cinderella tale I had dreamed of. Abuse was on-going from very early on. He would throw food, break dishes, send heavy tools across the room, break our kitchen table and our dining room chairs, and put his fist through the glass of the china cupboard. One time he actually beat me with a doll I had saved from childhood, striking me over and over again, and kicking me. He did not relent until the doll was broken into shreds.

Outside, he would attack me with hammers and farm tools. Even the barn fork and the barn scraper became attack tools. He would chase me with the tractors and the trucks, threatening to run me down. He would throw objects at my head and tackle me in football fashion, bringing me down on the frozen ground. He would try to choke me and drop kick my stomach like a professional wrestler. If I was trying to repair the cattle's electric fence, he would plug in in so that I would get a shock.

The verbal and emotional abuse went along and exceeded those many episodes. I was continually told how stupid I was, how inept I was, how I was doing tasks incorrectly. When the calves I was raising died, he called me, "Calf killer! Calf killer!" over and over again while denying me the ability to call the veterinarian. Since I was working as a teacher throughout our marriage, I was constantly told I was not earning enough money, or I was wasting money. He would even beat me if I looked at him in a way he interpreted as mean.

Why? I will never really know. When I was in seminary and was in the process of leaving and divorcing him, I studied brain chemistry, the atmosphere of his childhood, styles of discipline, inherited traits. Nothing really gave me the answer. The one thing that was obvious to me, however, was that he was in control of it. He would never beat or put me down in a public setting. But, as soon as we would be on the way home, the verbal and emotional abuse would start. I would be lucky if it would end there. Sometimes it would end in forced sex. Sometimes I would just cooperate to save myself from more hurtful physical abuse that might follow if I didn't.

As our girls were growing up, they were often subjected to verbal and emotional abuse. Put-downs were a constant. Criticism happened often. As the girls were getting older, physical abuse was getting closer to happening as he would threaten to strike them with a belt. At one point, when our oldest daughter was a toddler, Bob had slapped her so hard, she had a hand welt on her bare, two-year-old back.

Probably the most notable characteristic of Bob's abuse was the way he laughed when he had hurt me. This factor became especially clear to me as I listened to Christine Blasey-Ford's testimony preceding Brett Kavanaugh's ascent to the United States Supreme Court. When asked what she remembered most about his alleged, attempted rape, she said, "His laugh" as he did it. Bob was the same. As I limped away, nursed my wounds, wiped the manure off of my clothing, was pounded into a cement block wall, nearly choked with the scarf I wore doing chores, he would laugh. I can still hear that laugh if I focus inward on those events.

Although the abuse was present from the beginning of our marriage, at first it was sporadic. But, as time went on, it occurred more and more often. Towards our marriage's end, there were many instances of abuse several times a week. It had become a permanent fixture of the relationship. My sister had warned me that Bob would, unintentionally, end my life.

In 1995, the first time I called the sheriff's office, he was threatening our middle daughter with the buckle of the leather belt he had removed from his blue jeans. As I got up to defend her, he beat me hard, throwing me against the washer and dryer and kicking me. I called the sheriff's office that afternoon. I had, by that time, been in therapy for over a year due to the deep depression I fell into in the fall of 1993.

The sheriff and a deputy came and had both of us sit at our kitchen table. At that time the sheriff told me that Bob would "never do such a thing. I've (the sheriff) known him since high school." Then they left the farm.

Bob said, "See, I told you they wouldn't do anything!"

That was the July day I decided I would never be safe if I stayed in that rural area. In my mind, I began leaving. I just did not know how that would look as yet.

I attended my first year of seminary from 1995-1996 commuting the seventy-five miles from the farm to class and staying part time with a friend in the Twin Cities. I felt it necessary to remain on the farm during that school year. Bonnie was a senior in high school and would be graduating in the spring. Krista and Amy needed to finish their school years with their classes. But, in Spring, when a chance opened up to sub-lease an apartment for the summer, I jumped at my chance.

In the fall of 1996, when another year of classes was about to begin, I moved to my own apartment. Bonnie moved to the dormitory at the college she was attending. I had found a family from church with whom Krista could live until she finished high school. Amy, still in grade school, moved with me and began attending an elementary school near the seminary.

By November of that year (1996), things had gotten so tense with

Bob, that, when he physically threatened me, I filed for and received an Order for Protection. That winter, I did not go back to the farm unless absolutely necessary.

The following summer I sought out an attorney to ask about a divorce. It was my second visit to talk with him. But even though everything I have described had occurred, I was still having trouble making the decision to move ahead with the divorce, which I felt was against my faith.

By February of my third year in seminary, while I was doing my internship, I decided to move ahead with the divorce. On Valentine's day of 1998, I filed the divorce papers with the attorney. On May 28, 1998, I left the courtroom of the county in which the farm was located a free woman. That did not totally end our relationship, however.

Although my marriage to Bob was characterized by abuse, we also had good times, and we were alike in many ways. We were both fairly conservative in our finances. We were able to work together with the cattle and the machinery in very cohesive and cooperative ways when everything was going well, which was more often than not. We both had our farm duties and were able to divide fairly equitably what was an enormous amount of work. We enjoyed friends together, shared experiences with 4-H families in the club to which the girls and their friends belonged. Bob enjoyed playing softball, and I enjoyed visiting with the women while he did so. Both of us enjoyed being with our own families, although he enjoyed his family, which was quite large, more than he enjoyed mine. And, we went to church together. He served as the treasurer and church board member while I taught Sunday School, was active in the women's groups, and served on the Parish Board of Education. I thought we shared the same faith.

Bob was not supportive of my endeavors, however. In over twenty years of teaching, I was never asked how my day had gone. Although he bragged of my artistic talents in public, he chided me that they were a complete waste of time in private. In fact, in over twenty years of marriage, I was never allowed to paint any canvas even though one of my degrees was in art. He did allow me to sew, however, which was something in which I had very advanced skills. But that was merely to save us money. He never complimented me on anything that I had made. Although I kept the yard neat and clean, repaired cattle fences, unloaded and stacked hay bales, bought, washed, and chose all of his clothes, there was never a thank you.

Despite all that, we were very connected. I think the responsibilities of the farm and our ability to work well together, in spite of the elements and tasks, bound us in a way perhaps a couple living in town or in the city would not be connected. Even though I don't think he ever was able to reach out to truly understand me, I understood him and what pleased him very well.

He was also not supportive monetarily. He thought all money earned through the farm work was to go back into the farm. Part of what contributed to that was the fact that the farm, despite ongoing and unrelenting work, barely, if ever, turned a profit. If he was going to buy or replace needed machinery, it would take all the income he could generate. Of course, I was helping him generate that income and getting nothing for my work. That left my teaching income to support the household and the family. There was just nothing ever left over. He was a hard worker, however. He did not drink or party. And, he was never involved with other women. So, there was enough to our marriage to hold it together longer than it would have probably otherwise survived.

Because Bob was an abuser, and I had an Order for Protection against him, he was not allowed to attend the divorce proceeding in the courtroom unless he hired an attorney. He did not. So, it was just my attorney and I along with the judge, the sheriff's deputy, (who had agreed that Bob had not beaten me that July day in 1995), and a few other court people. All I asked for in the divorce was a small portion of the value of the land. I didn't ask for half of it. I didn't ask for any of the value of the cattle, crops, grain we had stored, hay and straw bales, cattle sileage, tools and supplies, or machinery. I wanted Bob to be able to pay what he owed me without having to sell the cows or the farm. If he had to sell out because of the divorce, he would have constantly been on my doorstep, and I knew it. Besides, when he feared that I was leaving (which I, indeed, was), he had said to me, "If you try to leave, I will kill you!" He had nearly done that often enough. I believed that he would have. Luckily, with my degrees and training, I would be able to support myself. And I did.

Bob made no attempt to have custody of the girls. He did not want custody. Although he wanted to share in their successes and achievements, he did not want any of the responsibilities for their care. Bonnie, who was already over 18 when I left, was on her own. Because Krista was not living with me, I received no child support for her care. Between her own earnings from work at a convenience store and what little I had to give her, she survived until she graduated from high school. Bob was forced to pay child support for Amy. Even at that, having hid most of his income to save on paying taxes, he paid the least possible. Two hundred and thirty-seven dollars a month did not go far. It did not even cover Amy's extracurricular activities and school fees, much less clothing, food, and housing.

Even with these factors being true, I experienced some sadness in the loss of the marriage. At first, I missed the farm. That changed with time. I missed having someone off of which I could bounce ideas. Even though my youngest daughter was with me, I could not share with her like one shares with a marriage partner. I missed the sense of "us," even though "us" had been downright dangerous at times. I had had hopes for a loving marriage, with many happy, shared memories. That dream had been crushed. I grieved that loss.

After the divorce and with my fear of him, we had very little to do with each other for nearly five years. Occasionally, there was a family event that would bring us to the same place at the same time. One such occasion was our oldest daughter, Bonnie's, college graduation.

Also, there were Krista's graduations with her Legal Secretary degree and, later, her Bachelor of Arts degree. He was not allowed at my seminary graduation or my ordination into ministry. He was not allowed at Amy's confirmation. He rarely was allowed at any of Amy's concerts or athletic events while in junior high school or senior high school. He did, however, attend Amy's high school graduation and her graduation with her Bachelor and Master degrees from college.

As time went on, I came to trust Bob more. He was not showing abusive tendencies when we attended events together. It did seem he was becoming more docile. That was probably due partly to his wanting to have interaction with his family, especially when each of the girls got married. He did not, however, walk them down the aisle at their weddings.

Later, I allowed Bob to ride with me to family events. We attended baptisms and birthday parties riding together. We flew together to Bonnie's wedding in Indiana and stayed in the same apartment during our stay there (in separate bedrooms, of course). I guess I would say we had developed a type of relationship of cordiality, a way of "getting along" that grew out of knowing each other very well having been married. We certainly did not agree on everything, but we were able to converse without conflict. Sometimes I could calm him when he was upset about something, just the same as I had often done when I had been married to him. He helped me do some outdoor painting when I was readying my house for sale. He helped me move to my condo. He called me just to talk every so often. It was more than simple toleration, but I would not call the relationship one of friendship either. We were able to talk and spend time together without any conflict—until the night of the fight at Amy's cabin that last Labor Day of his life.

Many perhaps are wondering how I could interact with Bob and allow him in my life in any way after what he had done to me and the way he had treated me during our marriage. I guess I saw him as someone, who had some severe mental and emotional issues. Although these did not seem too significant when I married him, they increased and began to greatly influence his behavior over time.

Bob had very high anxiety. His anxiety would overtake his ability to control his behavior when aspects of farming, which were mostly out of his control, did not work out as planned. At first, he would merely rub his hands together quickly to work the anxiety out of his system. Over time, the only way he rid himself of the excess and extreme anxiety was to lash out verbally or physically on those of us he was supposed to be (and I believe he did love as he was able) loving. Hence, if the hay was not drying because of on-going humidity and cloudy skies, a pitcher of Kool-Aid might get dumped over my head. If the cattle got sick because of muddy manure on the feeding platform, a pitchfork might fly my way. If a piece of machinery broke down, which was fairly common due to our machinery being quite old, a wrench could come flying and hit me in the knee. If the corn and soybeans drowned out because of flooding rains, he would holler at the kids until they were in tears. His anxiety and his abusive behavior were inextricably tied.

As someone, who worked with disabled clients during my twenty-one-year teaching career, I also observed other behavioral issues. He was a narcissist. He needed constant attention, constant praise, to feel good about himself. He needed me to mirror his comments back to him for validation.

He often referred to himself in the third person voice,

"Bob's corn is the best in the neighborhood!"

"Bob's crop rows are straighter than _____'s!"

"Bob has it harder than anyone else!"

When I would say to him that he was acting like a baby, he would respond, "I am the baby!" Although he was the youngest child in his family by far with his next closest sister ten years older than him, in our family he was not the "baby." He was the "head" of our family. I would point that out at those times. But he never quit identifying himself as "the baby."

As I have talked with mental health professionals during my own therapy after leaving the marriage, and as I have described some of the things he would say or ways he would react or behave, they have said that it sounded like he had an antisocial, borderline personality disorder. This became ever more evident and inappropriate through time to the point at which time it was impossible and dangerous to live with him. I said this in his funeral sermon:

"Once we returned to the farm (after college and our marriage), things gradually began to change. I can't explain the mental, social, and behavioral deterioration that occurred at first slowly, and, in these later years and weeks, more rapidly. A definite mental deterioration was present, whether by choice or not. He could never bring himself to say he was sorry, to me or to our daughters. I think his giving up on the care of the farm was part of that. And he did try doing things for us, even helping me move in July."

He had become erratic and dangerous to me and our girls in the almost twenty-four years of our marriage. So, I had no choice but to leave and to make sure our daughters were safe.

Although I cannot say that I "missed" him after his death, because of the time we spent working on tasks on the farm and doing things together as years passed after the divorce, the death in some way did put a "hole" in the life I had gotten used to in his regard.

CHAPTER 7

Letting Go

ALTHOUGH THE GIRLS and I were all moved in some way by Bob's fairly sudden passing, there were not many tears. Although the girls may have had a few tears the day of the funeral, I felt no sadness that day. Perhaps I was matter of fact, having walked that last month of his life with him. I think I partially went into "pastor mode." As a pastor, I had learned to separate my emotions from my duties the day of someone's funeral. This was necessary in order to properly lead the memorial service and treat the affair with the dignity it deserved. I might break down after my duties were finished, especially if I had developed a meaningful relationship with the person for whom I was doing the service.

I did not break down the day of Bob's funeral though. As I said, I had a relationship of sorts with him, but it was not a close relationship of friendship. It was more of a relationship of helping him with things for which he needed my help. Also, the activity of the day following the funeral, moving from visitation, to funeral, to lunch, to committal, to cleaning up the farm, pushed me through the day experiencing very little feeling. The greetings, friendship, and hugs from so many, both relatives and friends, whom I had not seen for such a long time, were actually uplifting. When I had left the marriage, I think people were confused, so I received very little support. As Bob's mental, emotional, and social abilities appeared to deteriorate after I left, I think people began to understand the issues which had contributed to my leaving. I was now accepted. I was welcomed. That felt very good to me.

Although I experienced a sense of disorientation the day after the funeral weekend when I was back in the Twin Cities by myself, it was not until November when a sadness of sorts set in. The sadness was not really missing Bob, but a different feeling. Melancholy maybe. I felt like I had been in shock and was just starting to come out of it. At that time, Krista asked me if I was missing his phone calls, at which times he was often upset at something and would calm as I spoke with him. I did not miss those phone calls at all, not even once.

Did I miss Bob being at grandchildren's birthday parties? Not at all. The girls did not either. In fact, they often said how nice it was that their father was not at those events talking constantly about something about which they did not care. I drove out to those parties by myself, not constrained by his schedule or behavior.

Did I or the girls and their families miss Bob at our family's gathering for Christmas the year following his death? No. We, his family, celebrated together in the party room of my condo building. It was busy with so many young children. And, with the children, there was a real sense of joy in the air. Everyone brought food. I made chili to share. We celebrated by eating and, then, opening gifts. Bonnie's husband, Kevin, gave horsey rides on his back, which were a hit with the kids, especially Maggie, who scampered up onto the piano bench in the room to climb aboard Kevin's back.

I think I did experience a sense of shock, however, following Bob's tumor ordeal and subsequent, quick death. It had occurred over a relatively short time; one month. A tumor, which would lead to death, was the last thing I was expecting. I hadn't even entertained the thought that he would not live. Then the farm clean-up had all happened so quickly.

On only a few occasions had I been back to the farm or in the farmhouse during the years after I had left. I had left almost everything behind—my dishes, my furniture, wall decorations and pictures I did not want to take—all of it reminders of all that had transpired there. So, even though the farmhouse was extremely dirty, going into the farmhouse was, in a way, like stepping back into the time I had lived there. Everything was sitting or hanging the way I had left it, except for the turned-over furniture. It was still in a sense "my house." As I walked through it, it took me back to both pleasant and unpleasant memories I had long put out of my mind. It was a visit into my past. I am not sure I was ready to deal with those memories. And, I had not thought ahead of time that I would be feeling them. So, to say I was unprepared for the "flood" that came over me would be putting it mildly.

In late November, Bonnie was home. She and Amy decided they wanted to go out to the cemetery where Bob was buried and have one last walk around the farm before it was sold. They asked if I want-ed to ride along. So I went along.

It was mid-afternoon by the time we arrived at the cemetery with that late November, golden glow. The sun, halfway down in the west-ern sky, shone just above the row of evergreen trees into which the butterfly had flown that late September day when we buried Bob. The wind was blowing fairly briskly as it is apt to do out in prairie country, so the grass, which was left growing rather long this late in the year, was ruffled by the wind. The corn field, which had surrounded the cemetery in September, was gone, replaced with dark, black, plow ground.

There was a sense of "holiness" in the "vacantness" of the space. I allowed the girls to spend as much time there as they wanted, pe-rusing the stones of relatives, who had died before they were born. It was a holy walk.

We then drove to the abandoned farmyard, left clean and cleared by the crew of men, who had been working so hard at it when I was out in October. The machinery and the wagons of tires and scrap iron had been hauled away. The snow-fence corn crib, that I had given the men permission to remove to have the large, long posts, had been taken down. Everything seemed so open, so empty, so abandoned—so dead. Yet, I saw it as it had been when I had struggled for existence there. A barn with cattle noises within it. A tractor ready to run an elevator for unloading hay bales into the hay barn. Young calves bleating from the old, chicken barn we had turned into a calf barn, which had, in turn, burned down in 1997. Kids playing in the yard or swimming in the large, round stock tank, a purchase for their swimming pool. The farm dogs coming to greet us. In my memory, all of those images still exist to this day. But the absence of the farm's machinery, no cattle mulling around, no vehicles parked haphazardly, and no freshly-harvested corn in the cribs, spoke loudly that the owner—the proprietor—was no longer alive. And the farm had, in its own sense, also died.

The girls and I took one last walk through the farmhouse. Since it was no longer heated, it was cold now with late fall having arrived. Everything was as it had been left that first day of October when all of us, Bob's family, had left for our respective lives. It was dirty and empty. A bit of a cold breeze filtered through the rotting windows.

The girls went upstairs to take a last walk through what had been their bedrooms for so many years. I heard them slowly and methodically walk through those rooms. But I did not go upstairs. Seeing the downstairs so abandoned and feeling the cold of winter setting in within it moved me so deeply, I had had enough of the experience. The girls came back down the stairs. We exited the house with Bonnie locking the door behind us. Very little was spoken. The experience was emotionally moving for all of us.

As Amy was turning the car around to leave, I took one last look towards the house. It was then that I noticed the three, wooden butterflies I had attached to the frame of the entry window thirty years before. I had splurged in purchasing them from a man in Arlington, who made and painted them in bright colors. I had chosen the bright, red ones to match the red trim on our white farmhouse. Now, all the paint was gone. All the color was gone. Yet, they remained attached to the window frame. Perhaps their lack of paint was a sign of the death of our marriage, as well as Bob's death. But, then, maybe the three of them, still alighting the window frame, were a sign that, in the end, life triumphs over death, and that hope and a future are always promised.

We stopped at the road crossing just to the northeast of the farm, posing ahead of the stop sign, with the full view of the farmyard and the plow fields behind us. Bonnie's husband, Kevin, took a picture of me with Bonnie and Amy. We then climbed into Amy's vehicle and left. We had said our final good-bye.

Conversation on the way back to the Twin Cities and a late lunch at a restaurant in Eden Prairie lightened our moods. Bonnie and Kevin headed to the airport. Amy headed back to her home and family. I went back inside of my condo. It was then that I wrote the poem, "That I Must Grieve You Twice." [APPENDIX II] I needed to pour out all of the memories, all of the feelings, all of the grief over both my life with Bob, and now, my life beyond his death. The words flowed onto the paper. And, whatever feeling of sadness or melancholy I had been experiencing, went away. I was letting go.

CHAPTER 8

These Questions

LOOKING BACK AT the events surrounding the last month of Bob's life and, most notably, the last week and a half, there are questions that now I wished I would have asked but did not.

The first ones surround some of his last actions and comments when I had picked him up at the farm in order to have him at the hospital for surgery the next morning. As I said earlier, instead of climbing immediately into my car when I arrived at the farm, he circled with his body, saying, "In case I never see all this again." What was he thinking?

Once at the post office, there was a long pause when he had been asked how long he wanted his mail to be forwarded to my address. It was a pregnant moment's pause. What was he thinking?

As we headed northeast out of Arlington towards the Twin Cities, when speaking of his bus driving job, Bob said emphatically, "I'm coming back." And repeated it, "I'm coming back." I looked at him and observed the consternation on his face. Why didn't I ask, "Do you think that you might not?" But I said nothing.

About halfway to the Twin Cities, Bob mentioned a comment spoken to him by an Arlington resident in the grocery store when he had told her what was happening with him. He said, "I told her that I have a brain tumor and that I was going for surgery on Thursday."

She said, "Everybody has to die sometime."

I responded, "She would know the feeling. She's been close to death often enough." This woman had had a recurrence of breast cancer, so certainly knew the uncertainty of living from scan to scan not knowing if the cancer had returned.

I wish I would have asked him, "Do you think that you're going to die? What do you think about that? How does that feel to you? What does it mean to be facing your own death?" I could have engaged him about his thoughts on death. Although he was not one to explore those things on his own, as a pastor, I could have encouraged him to express his concerns and worries. It would have perhaps helped him to verbalize what he had in his thoughts during that drive.

I did not ask him partly, I think, because, even though he was indicating he was having thoughts about his own death, my mind had not gone there. As I have said before, I had never even entertained the possibility. Even as he seemed to be having some doubts, in my mind, I was sure that the doctors would fix him. He would be back to normal. Or so I thought.

That evening, when he complimented me on the smell of dinner and the goodness of the chicken, I could have asked, "Why are you complimenting me now? You never complimented me all those years I cooked for you on the farm." I did not encourage conversation surrounding those compliments. What was he thinking? Why did he notice those things at this time? What was he really trying to say?

The next morning, he complimented me again. He stated, "It sure sleeps good on your couch! I really slept!"

I could have asked, "You've slept on my couch before. Did it sleep better this time than the other times? Why are you complimenting me on that now?" Again, I failed to ask him where the compliment was coming from.

When Krista went to visit Bob on the Saturday between his two brain surgeries, she said that there was no substance to his conversation. She said, "Mom, I asked him how they (the surgeon and nurses) were going to remove the tumor? I asked him what they said about it?" She *did* ask him about his surgery. She asked what the doctors were going to do? He merely answered, "I don't want to know."

Perhaps more questioning, perhaps by calling a nurse in to assist in the conversation, he would have opened up a bit. I think that would have been helpful to him. But then, maybe not.

But, again, in my mind, I never gave the possibility of his dying the light of day.

A second area of questioning could have been between me and the nurse practitioner.

When she mentioned to me that we might benefit from genetic counseling, I could have asked her more about Bob's condition. "What kind of tumor does he have? What caused it? Is it something that just grows on its own for no apparent reason? What is genetic counseling? How does that apply to our family? What do we need to be concerned about going forward?"—among other questions.

After Bob was dead and buried, I had all kinds of questions that the nurse practitioner could have answered. Perhaps we, as a family, if we had known what type of tumor Bob had, could have scheduled a genetic counseling session. She had, in passing, called it a Von-Hippel Lindau tumor. I had no idea what that was. Why didn't I ask? Instead, after the funeral and everything had settled down, I wanted to know the answers to these questions. I turned to Google, looking up Von-Hippel Lindau brain tumors. This is what I learned.

Von-Hippel Lindau tumors are very rare, only affecting about two percent of the population. Von-Hippel Lindau brain tumors are vascular tumors occurring in the cerebellum. They are masses of intrusive cells that grow and thrive being fed by blood vessels and arteries. The better they are fed, the larger they grow. The measurements of Bob's mass were printed on the paper I had given the doctor in the emergency ward that first night I had taken him to Abbott. I didn't look closely at those measurements. Instead I tried to digest what the imaging department had termed "large mass." Although that tumor may have been growing for a long time, I am sure the seven months between February, when Bob first started complaining of symptoms, and that later time, when I insisted that he have his symptoms checked out at the end of August, did not help.

The article on Google said that Von Hippel Lindau tumors can grow fairly fast, especially if they are well-fed. Bob had no artery blockages, so, indeed, his tumor was well-nourished.

Von Hippel-Lindau tumors, I learned, are caused by two mutant genes. One of those mutant genes is present at birth. Thus, they are hereditary. That is the genetic component. The second gene must mutate in order for tumors to develop. What had caused Bob's second gene to mutate is unknown. We will never know the answer to that question. Was it an injury—perhaps a head injury? Was it all the spraying of poisonous herbicides and pesticides he had applied to farmers' fields as a college student while working summers for a local agricultural plant? Was it all the fly spray we were constantly spraying in our cattle barn during the summers to keep the flies away from the cattle? Or was it none of those things? We will never know.

Often, with Von Hippel-Lindau tumors, there are "mini tumors" going down the brainstem, which have not yet developed into a tumorous mass large enough to see on a brain scan. That evidently was the case with Bob as the brain surgeon indicated. One of those small tumors was likely the cause of the bleed that caused the stroke into the cavern left by removal of the large tumor. In that case, as I have said before, he would have likely experienced tumor following tumor for the rest of his life—a life of constant tumor removal and rehabilitation.

Von-Hippel Lindau tumors occur most often in males in families. I thought about Bob's many uncles, who had now passed away. Looking back at least two generations, I was not aware that any of the males had died of a brain tumor. So, I have no idea how or when this malady had shown itself in Bob's lineage.

Since Bob and I had three daughters, it is unlikely our girls will suffer this condition. But they could be carriers. I have four grandsons. Will any of them suffer a fate similar to Bob's? Only time will really tell. The condition may not reappear again for several generations. Those who experience it then will not have to wonder as we do. We will have a written record of its existence.

What our grandsons and the males, who follow them, will have to their benefit is that we know this condition can exist in our family now. So, if any of the boys suffer similar symptoms at some time in their life, our family will know what they might suspect. Also, going forward, medical science is constantly learning more and improving on treatments. If our grandsons or generations to follow develop such tumors as adult men, perhaps surgeries or treatments will have improved. And, perhaps it will be generations before the condition reoccurs. Only time will tell. Perhaps the knowledge we have gained through Bob's tumor will save someone's life down the road. Perhaps, then, Bob will not have died in vain.

If I had known these things when the nurse practitioner suggested genetic counseling, I am pretty sure our family would have decided to do it. But, not having received it, at least we know what we know. We are armed with useful information. Hopefully, this will be helpful going forward.

Because the tumor was located in Bob's cerebellum, I read up on tumors of the cerebellum. It was late one night when I was searching this on my smart phone in the darkness of my bedroom. It was then that I read that tumors of the cerebellum can affect language. That made me pause. I felt a terrible sense of guilt pour over me.

When Bob made that sign to me the day after the tumor was removed, the sign in which he circled his head and made a talking sign with his thumb and fingers, I now was sure I had read the sign incorrectly. He circled his head before he made the talking sign. I had read it that, because of my talking, his head was hurting. I am quite sure instead he was saying, "Because of my head surgery, I can't talk." And he signed again, "Because of my head surgery, I can't talk."

I had said what I said so quickly and left so abruptly not looking back, I did not give him a chance to show me that I was misinterpreting him. I could have paused. I could have asked, "I'm not sure what you mean. Can you tell me again?" I could have stayed to allow him to let me figure it out accurately. But I did not. I left. That was my last interaction with him.

As I write now, I think of a phone call I had had from a friend a few years earlier, who was speaking to me about her husband's recent death. She had confessed to me, "I said something mean that I shouldn't have said to him. But I didn't think he was going to die!"

As a pastor I recommended that she not blame herself for being human in a stressful situation. "You can't blame yourself. You couldn't know. You are human. Sometimes we say things we don't really mean. You need to give yourself grace just as God gives grace to you."

When my misinterpretation of Bob's sign comes to mind and weighs heavily on me, I have to listen to my own words. When I feel guilty that I did not engage Bob but so quickly left his room and the hospital, I have to take in my own words. When I guilt myself, since my misinterpretation was my last interaction with Bob, I have to grant myself grace just as God gives me grace. Even though I am a pastor, I make mistakes. I say and do things I do not mean. I am human just like everyone else. And, how could I have known?

Finally, I had a question I addressed to a cousin of mine. I had just attended my godmother's funeral five months after Bob's. As we were leaving the committal service, I asked, "Do you think I was wrong in pushing Bob to see the doctor? I'm sure he would have lived longer if he would not have seen the doctor, had not had the surgery to remove the tumor." I was feeling guilt for, perhaps, quickening Bob's death even though I knew why I had done so.

I remembered the panic that went through me as I lay in bed the night before I called Bob directing him to go to the doctor. I had panicked that night as I thought of the possibility of him taking a bus load of school kids or athletes down with him should he have another bleed like the one he had told me he had had. My cousin had been present at his funeral at the end of September as I preached these words:

"He experienced a severe headache and bleed into his eye socket and from his nose and mouth about a month ago. Three days later, when he was telling me about this, I was like, 'You've got to go to the doctor! This could happen again, and it could be fatal!' . . . In the meantime, he was driving sports teams and teachers' training trips. My fear, that I expressed to him, was that, if he didn't seek help, he could take a whole busload of kids down with him. The CAT scan set in motion the whole series of events, which has brought us to this day."

My cousin assured me that I was up against the start of a new school year. He said, "You had to do what you did. If he had continued driving bus, kids could have been killed. School was about to start. You had to act."

I had taken the only action I could take to prevent the deaths of his riders since he seemed unwilling to stop driving bus on his own. I encouraged him and actively enabled him to get treatment. In actuality, I "ordered" him to get medical treatment!

Even when we take the only actions available when we are faced with a difficult situation, we may second guess ourselves. We may feel guilt. Then it is good to ask the questions. I am glad I did push myself to ask that question and raise that concern. Now I can more peaceably live with myself. I did what I could.

CHAPTER 9

Unconscious Rumblings

AS A FORMER abused wife, I suffer from depression, anxiety, panic attacks, and, most notably, Post Traumatic Stress Disorder (PTSD). Although some aspects of PTSD, such as hypervigilance and an exaggerated panic response, occur regularly, the nightmares and flashbacks are the most disruptive and unsettling. Tim O'Brien described PTSD in his book, The Things They Carried, detailing his experience and that of his platoon during the war in Vietnam and, then, the difficulty upon returning home. He wrote that twenty years later (after being free of the situation of cause), he would wake up watching the story happen in his head. "The bad stuff never stops happening. It lives in its own dimension, replaying itself over and over." (O'Brien, Tim, The Things They Carried, Mariner Books: Houghton, Mifflin, Harcourt: Boston/New York, 1990, p.31). For me, PTSD shows itself most often, but not exclusively, in my dreams. These dreams continued and actually increased in the two and a half years following Bob's death.

As I journaled during the time following Bob's death, I recorded the content of a dream I had near the one-year anniversary of his death, which took me back to when we were grinding feed for the cattle. It had rained heavily, so there was standing water in the area around our place of work into which, inevitably, cobs of field corn fell instead of going into the feed grinder. After Bob raced off to unload the feed into the feed room, I stayed back pulling water-soaked corn cobs out of the slush and piling them on the dryer ground.

In my dream, after that, we joined the girls in the house, where piles of dirty dishes were waiting to be washed and dried. I washed and washed and washed in my dream, but there seemed to be an endless supply of the gold, plastic, cereal bowls we used in those early days of our married life.

It was getting to be time to feed the cows and prepare for the chore of evening milking. Bob was scolding me to get outside and do that feeding. I asked him to dry some of the bowls to speed up my task so I could get outside in a timely manner. He bluntly refused saying that he did not do "women's work!" The stack of washed bowls then toppled over the dish rack and onto the floor. It was then that I awoke, feeling the full brunt of his comment.

On November 22, 2018, I woke from another nightmare and wrote that I was trying to feed the cows hay bales in my dream. I was feeding them in the barn because the feedlot outside was all mud—thigh, high mud. I wrote;

> I had to get the bales from the shed with the John Deere tractor loader. I had to make many trips because, when the loader on the tractor got too heavy, the back tires would just spin down into the soupy mess. I fed what I thought were the right ones, but they were not. When Bob saw this, he exploded and lunged forward to tackle me. He laughed as I picked myself up from the mud."

I woke up in a fright and could not get back to sleep. My heart was racing. I had to walk around to get myself calmed down.

Near Christmas, I journaled about another dream. Again, I was back on the farm taking care of the young cattle, as had been my job during our marriage. It had rained torrentially, as it often did. The cattle in the outside pens were halfway up to their bellies in muddy soup. Their hay, which I was throwing into their pens so they could eat, was soaked.

I turned from their care to the barn housing the baby calves. All of the baby calves had their heads in their feed bunk eating the ground corn I had given them. I went down the row of baby calf heads naming each one as I scanned them—Henry, Herman, Doris, Brenda, Sam. No Sam! Had he gotten out in the rainstorm? He was not eating. He was not even in the pen. Where had Sam gone? I turned to exit the door to look for him.

In my dream I then heard the words I had so often heard from my husband when the young stock were sick and dying in rainy, muddy, wet years just as it was in this dream, "Calf killer! Calf Killer!" At his shouting, I suddenly woke up. Although, as I got my bearings in the dark of the night, and I realized it was just a dream, and also, that I was nowhere near our farm or sick and missing cattle, the mean-spirited, shouted words to me in my dream seemed real. I had to calm myself down in order to get back to sleep.

On January 31, 2018, I journaled of another dream:

"In my dream, Bob was acting so immature. He was us-ing 'boys' locker room talk. He was saying, in his own filthy language, how all of the work in the house and taking care of the girls was women's work so he wouldn't do it even if ask. As I tried to do the work, and hurry so that I could get outside to help him with his work, he started bouncing a basketball off of my head over and over again. I tried to stop him. He grabbed my left arm and started twisting it behind my back."

Again, I woke up with a racing heart. I grabbed my left arm to tell myself that it was only a dream, that I was not in the farmhouse now. He could no longer hurt me.

On March 9, 2018 at 4:24 a.m., I was done sleeping for the night. I was awakened in the midst of another dream. In that dream, the young heifers were out of their fence on a patch of weeds. It was early morning, and I was feeding them so that I could get done with my morning chores in order to get to work on time. The electric fence was down;

"I am rushing to get the fence back up while I have lured the heifers back into their pen with their morning feeding of ground corn and hay. I am rushing to get the maze of electric wire pieced together around broken, plastic, insulators, that are supposed to support the wire. The cold temperatures over the last winter have caused several insulators to break. There are sections of the fence that should be supported by an insulator but are not. Bob is in the area yelling—always yelling. I am naming supplies that he needs to pick up while I am at work—two kinds of insulators, T-posts, new wire—so the fence can be repaired properly. In my dream, he is complaining rather than listening. He is no help. I am trying to get a section of the fence fixed at a corner where the wooden, corner post is broken off. I am rushing. I have to get to work! I cannot be late—again!"

Then I woke up. A year and a half after his death—it was a dream! The PTSD caused by him and the farming conditions, by the balancing of a career in teaching with work on a dairy farm was still alive and well in my dreams. On June 14, 2018 I wrote, "When I wake up from one of those dreams, my bed is completely torn apart. The sheets are messed up between the quilt and the blankets. Today was one of those mornings." I still remember the sense of panic I felt as I woke that warm, summer morning.

Again, on September 25, 2019, two years after Bob's death I woke up from another dream:

"I woke up this morning from a dream. I was arguing with Bob about selling the cows. We had actually had this discussion/argument at one time. We had agreed before our wedding that we would farm for a while and, maybe, do something different down the road. The year of the flood on the farm (1993), I said, 'We can't do this anymore (knowing that I couldn't do it anymore).' He had shouted at me, 'We are never going to do anything else! This is all we are ever going to do!' My heart sank down my legs and through my feet that afternoon. I remember exactly the time of day and where we were standing when we had the discussion. I knew I did not love him anymore after that day." [APPENDIX VI]

There were many more dreams, which I could pull into my consciousness easily if I tried, but I do not try. While journaling the dreams helps me express and, thus, relieve the fear and frustration I am experiencing during each dream, re-experiencing the dreams over again in my waking life can be crippling.

The afternoon that we had had the discussion about continuing to farm or not was in the nineteenth year of our marriage. I had just returned from work and was changing into my chore's shirt and jeans. The fields lay like large lakes with growing crops or weeds sticking over the water. The air was humid, and it was cloudy, signaling more rain to come.

Physically, I did not leave at that time. But, mentally and emotionally, I was gone. I just had to figure out how to make the physical leaving a reality. I continued to do the work necessary to keep the farm going for another two years as I continued my teaching job. Once I started my seminary studies, I commuted to seminary helping him with the farm work when I was at home. And, it would take another two years to actually seek the divorce.

The PTSD dreams, which have been present since I left the farm, increased dramatically in the months and years following Bob's death. My interaction with him through that time, and being re-exposed to the farm, the farmhouse, and the life I had there was still so vivid in my memory. Even now, I can pull up and picture those memories. I try hard not to do that.

The dreams, even now, always consist of broken machinery, sick cattle, trying to maintain cattle fences, trying to obtain feed for cattle in inclement weather, or trying to keep cattle from dying. They all take place in the context of torrential rains and lots and lots of mud. There is always a sense of being rushed because I need to get to work at my teaching job. And the consistent in all of them is Bob's anger and his attacks.

As I write now almost three years after his death, the dreams have subsided a bit. I hope they stay that way—far away! Yet, there are times when something in my world triggers a frightening or disturbing image from the past.

The night Amy and I left his room when the medical attendants had settled him in his ICU bed, I suffered one such past image. As we left the room, I felt a strong feeling of being disturbed by all of the medical attention Bob was receiving. I remembered all the times I or the girls needed medical attention, or to see the dentist, when he was very critical, even physically mean. At times he even prevented us from getting help. As I turned to leave, with my PTSD, I had a flashback of a time I really needed help, and he did everything in his power to prevent me from getting it. I felt extreme anger on this night as I left Abbott Hospital. Of course, the anger turned to tears, as it always does for me, by the time I reached my car. When I got home, I text the girls about this anger. Amy replied, "I was wondering what was going on because you had a blank stare on your face."

Another such PTSD image comes to mind now. When Krista was starting middle school, I was told, at a dental appointment for her, that she would need braces. I knew that there would be a very bad scene when we returned home, and I told Bob the news.

As I prepared supper, I broached the subject carefully, "The dentist says Krista needs braces. Her teeth are ready to have them put on now. I need to make an appointment at the orthodontist for her . . ."

I didn't get the entire sentence out before he started yelling, "And how do you think you're going to pay for that. She doesn't need braces. Those dentists just want to bleed us of our money. She's not going to get them. Do you know how many miles that's going to put on the car? Do you know all the gas that's going to take?" Bob shouted.

I would need to drive some distance to have the braces put on and maintained. And, I would need help paying for them. I had cried on the way home, but everyone in the family cried at his yelling. Bob hollered. He pushed me into the cupboards. He threw things. I bore the brunt of his angry punches. Yet, in the end, we sold two cows in order to make the payments. But I still have the image of that disturbance in my mind.

The images pop up in my mind, and I see them in my vision without warning when they are set off by life's circumstances. Most often, the images are out of my control. What is in my control is to breathe deeply through them, to walk them off, or to get busy with something I enjoy doing to push them into the background and leave them there, safely at a distance.

CHAPTER 10

To Forgive or Not to Forgive

PSYCHOLOGISTS GENERALLY DEFINE forgiveness as a conscious, deliberate decision to release feelings of resentment or vengeance toward someone who has caused you harm. It is the letting go of deeply held negative feelings.

An article on forgiveness published by U. C. Berkeley states, "Forgiveness is not glossing over or denying the seriousness of an offense against you . . . Instead, forgiveness brings the forgiver peace of mind and frees him or her from corrosive anger." (www.greatergood. Berkeley.edu.) This article also makes clear that forgiveness does not mean forgetting nor does it mean condoning or excusing the offense. Forgiveness does not obligate the forgiver to reconcile with the person, who has caused the harm, or release that person from legal accountability.

Fred Luskin, Director of Stanford University Forgiveness Projects, further defines the concept: "The essence of forgiveness is being resilient when things don't go the way you want, to be at peace with what is, be at peace with the vulnerability inherent in human life. Then you have to move forward and live your life without prejudice." Luskin says that the absence of prejudice informs forgiveness because the injured party can move forward and accept what is.

"Forgiveness allows the forgiver to let go of negative feelings, such as resentment or vengeance, allowing them to recognize their pain without letting that pain define them. This enables the forgiver to heal and move on with life. Forgiveness does not mean there will be reconciliation or release of legal account-ability. Forgiveness allows the forgiver to live free from anger and have peace of mind. (Luskin, Fred, "What is Forgiveness?", www. greatergood.berkely.edu., August 19, 2010)

Jerry Sittser, Professor of Religion at Whiteworth College, lost his mother, wife, and daughter in a car accident caused by a drunk driv-er. Somehow, in the court proceedings, the jury acquitted the drunk driver of the crime. He writes;

"I wanted revenge. I was beginning to hold hatred in my heart. I was edging toward becoming an unforgiving per-son and using what appeared to be the failure of the judi-cial system to justify my unforgiveness. I wanted to punish the wrongdoer and get even. The very thought of forgiveness seemed abhorrent to me. I realized at that moment that I had to forgive. If not, I would be consumed by my own unforgive-ness." (Sittser, Gerald, A Grace Disguised, Zondervan: Grand Rapids, Michigan, 2004, p. 135)

He continues that "revenge is like a fire that smolders in the bel-ly," (Ibid, p. 136) and that "unforgiveness is a temptation that most people who have suffered loss face." (Ibid., p. 137) He states;

"The process of forgiveness begins when victims real-ize that nothing—not justice, or revenge, or anything else—can reverse the wrong done. . . It is the process of choosing life over death . . . stopping the cycle of destruction and, in the wake of the wrong done, do what is right . . . Though forgiveness appears to contradict what seems fair and right, forgiving people decide that they would rather live in a merciful universe than a fair one, for their sake as much as for anyone else's." (Ibid., p. 143)

In the Christian faith, forgiveness is a central theme. It speaks of God's forgiveness of the human race through the saving action of Jesus Christ. We are taught to forgive as God has forgiven us. Since I was raised in the Christian faith, from childhood, I had been taught that forgiveness was a necessary action in life. I continue to agree with that. That does not make it easy, however. Some passages that inform this view are:

Luke 6:37: "Forgive and you will be forgiven."
Luke 6:36: "Do not be overcome by evil, but overcome
    evil with good,"
Mark 11:25: "Whenever you stand praying, forgive . . ."
Romans 12:21: "Be merciful just as [God] is merciful."

Forgiveness is a major tenet throughout the Biblical record. It is particularly stressed in the New Testament appearing hundreds of times.

C. S. Lewis, renowned theologian of the early twentieth century, writes, "To be a Christian means to forgive the inexcusable, because God has forgiven the inexcusable in you." (Oporto, Tiffini, The Official C.S. Lewis Group, Facebook, September 7, 2020)

Many of the Biblical passages, including the Lord's Prayer, seem to make forgiveness sound like law: "Forgive us our trespasses as we forgive those who trespass against us." [Lord's Prayer], or "For if you forgive others their trespasses, your heavenly Father will also forgive you." [Matthew 6:14]

Corrie ten Boom turns what sounds like a command, which would be difficult for us to follow, into the grace of receiving what we need in order to be forgiving people. She states' "I discovered that it is not on our forgiveness any more than on our goodness that the world's healing begins, but on God's. When He tells us to love our enemies, He gives, along with the command, the love itself." (Ibid., p. 131) It is not on our own accord that we can forgive, but God's unconditional love gives us both the power and the will to forgive.

In the middle of the afternoon on the Tuesday following the surgery to remove Bob's tumor, after he had made that sign to me that I felt I had interpreted correctly, I was lying on my bed thinking about all that had transpired so far. I was specifically thinking about the fact that I had, unwittingly, let him back into my life, slowly at first, and more as time went by. I was thinking about how I had gotten involved in what was happening to him, health wise, now. I was thinking about the role I would play with Bob going forward. Specifically, as a pastor I suppose, I was thinking about forgiveness in relation to Bob because of my Christian faith and teachings.

I was thinking about some of the ways Bob had caused me such deep hurt—the physical injuries, the name-calling, the verbal put-downs, the emotional agony. I thought about some of the specific instances of deep pain. I thought about his refusal to support his family. I thought about the instances that caused me to fall into the deep depression in 1993 when all of Bob's abuse over the years flooded over my consciousness, like someone tipped a precariously balanced pitcher. I remember the events of that hot, humid day in July, which led me to call the sheriff's department. I remember that he was threatening the girls more and more as time went by. Into my "forgiveness" thoughts that day and the prayers that followed, I heard Peter's question to Jesus about forgiveness, and Jesus' teaching that followed. [Matthew 18:21-22]

Peter asked Jesus, "How many times are we to forgive, as many as seven times?"

Jesus answered, "As many as seven times seven (or seventy-seven times)."

Jesus teaching on forgiveness was that it is to be limitless. We are never "done" forgiving. As I preached on the day of Bob's funeral, I said:

"We are to forgive again, and again, and again, and again. I knew this, but I had always thought of forgiving separate offenses. That day God's message was clear to me: Sometimes we need to forgive the same offense or cluster of offenses over and over and over again. . . This extreme peace came over me that afternoon, and it has been present with me all the days since. . . The example of Jesus, even when hanging on the cross, confirms Jesus' teaching and modeling of forgiveness throughout his lifetime. We are to follow his example."

I had never thought of forgiveness in that way before. I would never have thought of it that day on my own. I had never thought that sometimes we have to forgive the same offense more than once as we try to live according to Jesus' teachings in this life. Even today, I have to work at forgiving Bob's cruelty each time the thoughts come up even as I have moved forward with my life.

Soon after Bob's death, when I was speaking about forgiveness with one of my physicians, who is also trained as a hospital chaplain, he said he felt atonement by the injuring person prior to forgiveness is a necessity. When Bob and I had been married, he never said he was sorry for any infraction he committed. When I would suggest to him that he needed to say he was sorry, he would retort, "I never have to say that I'm sorry because I never do anything wrong."

How do I, as the injured party, deal with that kind of response in light of Jesus' teachings? I told this physician that I felt a survivor had to "let go" of the injuries of the past that occurred. He felt "moving on" was a better way to state it because letting go seemed to indicate a "falling" of sorts. As a survivor of domestic abuse, I have felt that I had to "let go" and "fall" first before I was able to "move on." Maybe that is the only way that forgiveness in any way can occur.

Sheri Bessi-Eckert, MA Therapist, wrote a piece called <u>That One</u>:

"Be that one. That one who forgives when deep offense has been committed. That one who loves when no one else does. That one who gives kindness to those who are mean. Be that one who looks past the insult, instead seeing the pain that motivated it. That one who shines light upon those who sit in utter darkness. Because the impact of being that one runs far and wide. It brings healing to the wounded, joy to the sad, and hope to those in despair. Be that one." (Bessi-Eckert, Sherri, MA, The Wellness Universe Blog, Christianity Today, @ sheriseckert, Portland, OR, June 22, 2019)

Nelson Mandela, who spent so many years unfairly prisoned in South Africa for his efforts towards human equality for all people, said, "As I walked out the door toward the gate that would lead to my freedom, I knew if I didn't leave my bitterness and hatred behind, I'd still be in prison." (Facebook, Mindful Christianity Today, October 26, 2019)

Barbara Johnson further explains, "Forgiveness does not make you weak, it sets you free." (Facebook, October 8, 2020)

Likewise, Coretta Scott King. wife of civil rights activist, Dr. Martin Luther King, Jr., who was known for his efforts to lead and help bring change for racial inequality through peaceful methods, said, "Hate is too great a burden to bear. It injures the hater more than it injures the hated." (Parris, Leo, "Understanding Cultural Diversity in Today's Complex World", 2006, p.54) I choose to love in my life now because "hatred is too great a burden to bear."

As I was in the process of preparing to write this book, I watched a television program about the three young women in Ohio, whom Julian Castro had held in confinement in his house and repeatedly raped over a period of ten years. (20/20, ABCnews.com, January 3, 2020)

One of them, Michelle Knight, whom the reporter interviewed, stated that she forgives because otherwise it's like "living in chains." She has changed her name to Lily Rose Lee to break free of the tragedy and torment of those years of her life. She has begun a new and good life now in her freedom. Her advice is, "Don't let the darkness control your likes and your life." These are good words to live by for anyone abused or deeply hurt by another human being.

Charles L. Griswold, a philosophy professor at Boston University, in a New York Times article (Facebook, NYT, 2019) speaks of "unilateral" and "bilateral" forgiveness. In bilateral forgiveness, in order for a victim to truly let go of his or her anger, the perpetrator must first admit responsibility. With Bob, that never happened and would never happen. So bilateral forgiveness will never be a possibility. There is no longer an opportunity for atonement. How can you have forgiveness without atonement?

Unilateral forgiveness is when the injured party lets go of the hurt and/or anger without ever receiving an apology. In this case, Griswold says, the injured person must assess whether the situation actually calls for forgiveness. Maybe, instead, mercy is what's called for. Perhaps my interactions and help to Bob after our divorce and particularly those last weeks of his life were acts of mercy, given simply because he was a human being, who needed my help.

Jerry Sittser writes;

"Forgiveness is costly. Forgiving people must give up the right to get even, a right that is not so easy to relinquish. They must show mercy when their human sensibilities tell them to punish . . . Mercy does not abrogate justice; it transcends it. . . Forgiving people try to do what is right in the face of so much wrong." (Sittser, Gerald, <u>A Grace Disguised</u>, Zondervan: Grand Rapids, Michigan, 2004, p. 142-3)

Maybe I was able to extend mercy because Bob's life was not completely defined by his abuse of me and his verbal and emotional abuse of the girls. Two years after his funeral, I was thinking about the life I had shared with him remembering some of his good characteristics. He was one of the hardest workers of whom I know. He was faithful to me in terms of 'forsaking all others." He loved bus driving, and he was very good at it. The kids on the bus loved him, especially the little ones. Somehow, in doing so, he was able to control his abusive behaviors. He was extremely gifted in math, like a walking calculator. I remembered all those things a wife remembers—those discussions, both good and bad, working together towards a goal on the farm and achieving it, both the glory of "making it" and the sadness and fear of not "making it." I remembered the feeling of his body breathing next to mine.

But in our almost twenty-four years of marriage, Bob did not show any interest in getting me a birthday present or celebrating an anniversary. In all those years, I received one Christmas gift, a crock pot, in 1982, when Krista was two years old. One other Christmas, in 1988, he "allowed" me to buy myself a microwave oven. He never took me out for our anniversary or even showed that it was important.

I received one Valentine from him—in year twenty. I think Bonnie had helped him buy it. By then, I think he knew he was in danger of my leaving him. It was a Dairy Queen cake and a little stuffed bear that said "I love you" when the stomach was pressed. We ate the cake. But I did not take the bear with me when I left. I am assuming the girls threw it out with the rest of the trash after Bob's death. As I think of it now, I am thankful for Bonnie's efforts. It was just too little too late.

I had lived in the farmhouse with Bob for twenty-one years. During that time, I was never allowed to buy new carpeting of my own choice. The carpeting his parents had put in in the 1950's was all I ever had. The hole that had developed in it where it had simply disintegrated from age, I covered with a piece of furniture. That same carpeting, blackened and moldy, still stretched over those floors that day in November when the girls and I purveyed the empty farmhouse and locked up the door behind us for the last time.

The money I used to put in kitchen cabinets and add the entry rooms onto the house was all my own, earned through my teaching job and a loan from my parents. I had repaid that loan month by month, year by year, the same as I had paid off the hospital bill after our youngest daughter's birth—a third girl he "never wanted in the first place!"

The anniversaries, birthdays, and Valentine's Days went down the drain along with what we once had together. The house was just the house. When I left, I took very few items with me from the house. I did not and have not dwelt on the house and what I left in it. The rest is just water over the dam—or should I say water down through the sewer pipes. Then, of course, there are all the times of the abuse, which, in the end, along with the farm's unrelenting drudgery, made me flee.

In A Beautiful Soul it is written:

"It took me a long time to understand what it means to forgive someone. I always wondered how I could forgive someone who chose to hurt me. But, after a lot of soul searching, I realized that forgiveness is not about accepting or excusing their behavior. It's about letting it go and preventing their behavior from destroying my heart." (Facebook, A Beautiful Soul, October 7, 2019)

Jerry Sittser says, "Forgiveness is more of a process than an event, more of a movement within the soul than an action on the surface." (Sittser, Gerald, A Grace Disguised, Zondervan: Grand Rapids, Michigan, 2004, p. 144) He adds:

"Unforgiveness makes a person sick by projecting the same scene of pain into the soul day after day, as if it were a video that never stops. Every time the scene is replayed, he or she relives the pain and becomes angry and bitter all over again . . . Forgiveness requires that we refuse to play the videotape and put it on the shelf. We remember the painful loss; we are aware of who is responsible. But we do not play it over and over again." (Ibid., p. 144)

But Sittser makes it clear that forgiveness does not mean forgetting the wrong done. "Remembering the wrong done can make us a prisoner to pain and hatred, or it can make us the recipient of grace, love, and the healing power of God." (Ibid., p. 146)

I left Bob in year twenty-one while I still had my heart for caring for and about others. I divorced him in year twenty-four because I was finishing my ministry preparation and felt I needed to have the matter settled before serving my own parish. All the hopes and dreams I had had when I married were shattered. Even looking at his face at the time I left became intolerable. I left, not because I feared I could never forgive Bob, but because I was afraid that I would die without ever having really lived. And I grieved the loss of my marriage, the loss of a dream, and the loss of the life I had had until that point.

CHAPTER 11

And Then There Was Grief

AS A PASTOR, who often has done pastoral counseling, I have spent hours reading materials which describe the grieving process. Some experts have broken the process of grieving into stages. Although it was once believed that we move through grieving stages in a sequential order, most experts today agree that grief is not a sequential process but that we move among phases of grief vacillating back and forth within them. Gradually, over time, we are able to assimilate the death and move on with life albeit in an altered form. Such experts have named these phases or aspects in various ways. Some of these include: Denial, Anger, Bargaining, and, finally, Acceptance, Reintegration, and Moving Forward. Anger and depression may include emotional turmoil. Before acceptance, there may be a great deal of resistance. For some there may be a great deal of guilt and/ or self-blame or the event may trigger trauma. (Dr. John Brantner, Department of Psychiatry, University of Minnesota) [APPENDIX IV]

Each category may include many other grief feelings. Denial can include numbness, disbelief, disorganization, or shock. Anger may take the form of rage or even guilt. Depression may include tiredness, sadness, and mood swings. There may also be sleep and appetite disturbances, or a preoccupation with the image of the deceased. At this stage a person may have a lessened immune response and fall victim to colds or other respiratory diseases. A person may be especially sensitive to stimuli, be searching, yearning, and pining. Over time, these symptoms slowly become less intense. Acceptance may finally lead to assimilation and integration into life as it looks in a new way. The self may be redefined, energy increases, and a person develops a normal sense of the deceased and begins to focus on new relationships. (notes by Dr. Janice Nadeau, Grief Therapist, on Dr. John Brantner's Grief Model)

Again, a person may move back and forth through these phases and not in a sequential order. But, overall, a person's everyday life experience moves from a loss-oriented existence to a restoration-orientated life. (Stroebe and Schut, The Dual Process Model of Coping with Bereavement, Death Studies, 1999) [APPENDIX III]

As a pastor, I have sat with many families, who have been experiencing or have experienced the loss of a loved one. Besides being a steady presence of support in a difficult time, I have been able to reaffirm the feelings of grief that they have named in their own personal ways. Letting them guide the conversations has always been my mode of operation.

If the death was occurring in a home, I often refocused their attention on photos in an album or objects around their homes that produced happy thoughts of their time with the person, who was dying. I gave several hours of reviewing happy photos with an older woman in one of my congregations and her two adult children as her husband was slowly dying in the bed they had shared together. By doing that I was able to refocus the family, often leading them to tell me about a trip to the cabin, an anniversary party, a first home, the birth of a child rather than staring at the intense and labored breathing of the one dying.

In a hospital, a Psalm or Bible verse, a prayer, or a hug and holding a hand were helpful. Even then the survivors would often lead me down a path to a happier time and the joy that these people had shared together. These times of sharing were especially valuable in helping me to shape the Celebration of Life or Memorial Service I would be presiding over soon.

I did not come into spending Bob's "dying time" without experience. I was not supporting my own children as one, who had never personally observed death, or as one, who was not able to be with a family in a comforting way. Yet, this was different. This was a person with whom I had been a school classmate. This was a person I had pledged my life to at one time. This was a person I had lived with and loved at one time. This was the person I had made my children and my life with for over twenty years. He was my age mate with both of us having turned sixty-five that year. That very fact was not lost on me.

But I was divorced from Bob. I had fallen out of love with him. My life goals had changed. I had left the farm and created for myself a new life. Yet, I had been called on to help him in his suffering. I had pushed him to get help. I had driven him to the hospital. I was the one the surgeon and his nurse were informing and consulting with until Bonnie had had to make the call to remove the breathing tube.

Neither of us had remarried. That was a significant factor in our association with each other over the almost twenty years since our divorce. In a way, Bob had never really stopped leaning on me. I had allowed him to attend family events with me. I was not the ex-wife sitting in the back pew of my ex-husband's funeral while his new wife and the children he and I had made together were in the front pew at the funeral. No, I was sitting in that front pew. I was sitting with our girls and their husbands while our grandchildren, whom he had wanted to see grow up, crowded in around me. I had written his funeral service. I had preached his funeral sermon. I had chosen his burial plot and helped our girls with all of the arrangements. I had been drawn into all of it. Willingly, yes, willingly.

During the summer of my move to my new condo and Bob's diagnosis, illness, and death, I had been doing premarital counseling and presiding at weddings. I had been filling in for vacationing pastors for Sunday services, and had performed a baptism. I had taken on a limited number of duties because of my on-going, very low hemoglobin. Without the appropriate level of hemoglobin, I was not getting enough oxygen, and so, was very tired all the time. I would puff if I had to walk too far.

At the time of Bob's death, I had one last event to preside over. That was a fortieth anniversary renewal of marriage vows. That occurred in mid-October, three weeks after Bob's funeral.

The anniversary was a grand affair at a fancy, supper club. The bride was dressed in a beautiful, lace-and-beaded, wedding gown. The groom looked dapper in a gray suit. Their daughter was the maid-of-honor. And their grandchildren looked perfect in their fancy clothes as the flower girl and ring bearer. Under an arch of greens and flowers, they repeated vows they had written themselves. There was so much love in the room and between this couple. There was a level of love I did not ever remember having in my marriage.

In mid-April, the fortieth anniversary bride called and left me a message. Her husband had died. As soon as I received the message, I called her back inquiring what had happened. I had not been aware that her husband had been experiencing bladder cancer for some time. He had finally succumbed to it. He was sixty-five years old. She asked if I would preside over the memorial service. I agreed to with great gladness.

The day of the service, I arrived early to spend time with the family. I thought the wife was holding up very well greeting the people, who were arriving. She sat quietly during the service as I tried my best to capture her husband's life and the great love he had for her and her family. Even at the cemetery, with her family and friends around her, she was doing well.

Everyone at the committal service prayed together the Lord's Prayer, at which time I committed a loving husband, father, grandfather, and friend to the ground. The wife gave me a beautiful, red rose from the spray on his casket. I gave her a hug and told her, if she needed me, she should call.

About a month later, the woman did call. She was beside herself with grief. She was depressed and was unable to function. She was imagining things, unable to make decisions, and overwhelmingly sad. She was crying when she spoke to me on the phone. And she continued to cry as we talked. We agreed on a meeting time and place.

Before I met her, I bought a small, pewter cross that said, "You are always in my prayers." I gave it to her the day we met and talked. I felt it would be important for her to have as something of which she could hold in order to remember that she was not alone in her grief. I let her tell me about her loving husband, their life together, watching him die, and how "impossible" her life was now. She said she was unable to figure out what to do with his belongings.

I assured her that she was not alone. I would be there if she needed me. She had her daughter, her daughter's husband, and her grandchildren. She had her friends with whom she golfed. I told her there was no hurry to rid her house of her husband's things, and that if she gave herself more time, she would figure those things out. I made some suggestions to help her. Depression and sadness are classic signs of grief.

I met her again in the fall. She was doing better, but angry at her husband for "going and dying on me!" as she put it. She was starting to share his possessions with those people and places, who would be able to use them. She was counting on her daughter to handle her finances. She was starting to come to terms with her husband's death. Anger and acceptance are classic signs of grief. The trauma of having witnessed his dying was dissipating.

I met her one last time a year after her husband's death. She was doing quite well. She had given away most of her husband's possessions. She had traded his four-wheel-drive vehicle for a sedan that she loved. She had gone on a short vacation with her brother-in-law. In the process she had visited with an old friend. She was smiling as she told me this. She was functioning again. She had accepted the death and was reactivating in her life in new ways. We shared a hug. I trust now, two years after her husband's death, she is doing even better.

My father died suddenly of a heart attack the Friday before Thanksgiving of my senior year in seminary in 1998. My last interaction with him was in October of that year when I travelled out to my parents' farm to collect produce for a Harvest/Thanksgiving display at the church where I was doing my internship. He was vibrant and healthy.

I went into a fog the day I heard the news of his death. I stayed in that fog through the whole process of funeral planning, visitation, and funeral. I felt deep pain and sadness at the loss of him in my life. I wanted him to see me graduate and be ordained. I wanted him to be part of my new ministry life. It was not to be. His funeral was the Monday of Thanksgiving week.

The Wednesday night before Thanksgiving Day, I assisted with the worship service at my church. I felt like I was floating, like I was not grounded in what was going on. That feeling stayed with me through Advent and Christmas. In January I felt like I was starting to wake up. But the sadness continued through the spring. It took me a long time to assimilate the new reality without him. Grief is hard. The hard work takes time. I still miss him at times when I think of the love that I had for him and what a special person he was in my life. But I rest content in the beautiful memories I retain of him and his love for his family.

I did feel grief following Bob's death, but I did not feel the sadness that my forty-year bride felt. I did not love Bob. That saved me that deep sadness. The melancholy/sadness I did feel almost two months after his death were more a result of the trauma the entire episode caused for me. The course of events shocked me. In a way I felt disbelief. I wrote:

"Trauma, trauma, and more trauma! I felt nothing emotionally in those first weeks. I wasn't elated. I wasn't sad. I didn't cry. There wasn't joy. I was tired, so weary worn. I felt like I had been through the wringer of my old washing machine. I was satisfied to just sit and watch the days go from sunny and warm to cloudy and cool, with the sun hiding between intermittent clouds in November. The haziness that hung in the air also filled my head as well. . . There was no sadness. In a sense there was a feeling of unreality." (July 14, 2018)

Denial and trauma following a death may seem to make the world meaningless and overwhelming. Life may make no sense. But several experts on grief say that shock provides emotional protection from being overwhelmed all at once. Denial and shock are nature's way of letting in only as much as we can handle.

I think I was partially in shock the day of Bob's funeral because I felt nothing except the responsibility that I had for preaching and making the day go well. It was not until six weeks later, as I settled into the aspects of the coming winter, that I started to come out of the shock. The numbing was letting up. As it did so, I felt sad. I felt like I had been run over by a huge truck, like I had had a great sickness and was beginning to heal. Instead of being intense, the grief was long and low.

As I started to "wake up" so to say, I imagined seeing Bob in the casket again. It was then that I couldn't decide if he had had his beard. He rarely shaved it off. I asked the girls if they could remember. They did not know either. It was not a matter of real significance, but I had looked at him in the casket. I had observed how he laid with his three fingers up in the air. I had seen the scar on his right forehead from the placement of the drainage tube. I remember thinking he looked very young. But I could not remember if he had his beard. I finally decided that he did not as we had given the mortician a picture from Amy's wedding as a guide. He did not have his beard on that picture. No wonder he looked so young. The beard with its gray hairs was not present.

I have felt anger, not that Bob died, but that he involved me. I have felt anger in the two-and-a-half years since, but I have felt that more related to his actions in life rather than the fact that he died. His death made me aware of his unkind actions again. It had just been so unbelievable because I had never considered death as an outcome. I still do not understand why. His death did force me to evaluate my own feelings of mortality. That has been especially true since I am only three days younger than Bob. His death has made me reflect on the fact that now I am also in my sixties. Suddenly, death seems a likely reality, and it could come sooner than I have ever imagined before.

I was disoriented the weeks after Bob's death. My life as I knew it had been upset. I had trouble getting back on track of accomplishing anything and actually doing my work. There was a "timelessness" to the weeks. Gradually, I gathered the bunch of clothes he had brought, which I had thrown out into my sun porch the week after he died. I put it in a bag and took it to the Goodwill near me.

I was easily frustrated the days and weeks following Bob's death, short on patience, and easily depressed. Everything was too much on some days. On other days I was fine, but even then, it did not take much to set me off, even something so minor as a task not working right. Now, I have trouble imagining what it is like to lose a spouse or partner whom one really loves. Having that person's clothing around the house, in the closets, and in the drawers would be almost more than I could deal with. Luckily, I was receiving therapy at the time. I was able to talk all of these things through.

I did journal at that time, referring back to the wife, for whom I had done the fortieth anniversary vows, in terms of my grief:

> "I sat by the table across from her as she poured out her heart to me deep in grief. Little did she know any wisdom or kind words I could impart came from my own place of grief, me having borne mine longer than her. Just three weeks after my ex-husband's whole brain tumor event, she and her husband had celebrated their fortieth anniversary in such a fine way, renewing their vows, dressing the part in wedding finery, with flowers and food, music and friends. They had invited

me to preside over the whole event—the wedding service, the pronouncement of joy of their recommitting to each other with the full and certain knowledge of what life with the other was truly like, both the ups and downs that marriage brings. . . They knew little of what the few weeks before their celebration had held for me.—the confusion, the seeking closure, the empty feeling of having taken someone, who had, at one time, been part of my life to the hospital for a procedure and never having brought him home afterward. In many ways, it was helpful that I was still somewhat numb to what had recently occurred in my life. As a pastor, I could preside over the occasion like so many I had presided over before. I was present for the event. But it was too soon. My insides screamed. I felt like I had a wall around me, somewhat disconnected from the events." (July 6, 2018)

I continued:

"Now it was two months since I had buried half of that woman's partnership. Her husband's cancer had flared. And this time it was lethal. From her description of those last hours before his death, I could tell she was traumatized by the dying event itself. I could well relate to that. I knew that I, too, was traumatized by the sight of Bob coming out of the surgery to remove the tumor, and then, further traumatized by seeing him lying dead in his hospital bed—the same kind of trauma of which this woman spoke the day we met. Yes, I could relate to her at the level of the trauma of death. It was still fresh for me as well." (July 6, 2018)

After the last trip out to the farm in November, as I stated earlier, I wrote the poem, "That I Must Grieve You Twice," which helped me express all of the thoughts I was having surrounding Bob's death.

Soon after, I wrote, "Death Drew Near," expressing my thoughts on the death itself and the death's impact on my life. In a way, by Bob's death, I was completely free of him, something I had not be able to attain in the almost twenty years I had been divorced from him.

H. Norman Wright addresses this aspect of grief—the fact that it may bring relief:

"Sometimes the relief is relationship relief when you've lived with criticism, abuse, oppression, or anxiety. If you lived in a relationship where you were constantly threated, humiliated, and mistreated, relief is the natural result. . . Relief is not the same as saying you are glad your loved one is dead. It's more of the lifting of a burden that had no other way of changing. It's not a betrayal or disloyalty or a character fault in you. It's a normal response." (Wright, H. Norman, <u>Experiencing Grief</u>, B & H Publishing: Nashville, Tennessee, 2004, p.59)

Because of Bob's abuse of me during our marriage and an ongoing "complicated" relationship with him following our divorce, with him still being very needful of my help, my grief has been complicated with vacillating feelings from some form of sadness, relief, and numbness. H. Norman Wright also addresses complicated grief:

"When a relationship has been difficult over the years, many end up feeling as if they were living a lie. They put on a positive face for years and lied to others but also lied to themselves about their own needs. When death is a relief, grievers may not have the opportunity to process their grief in the way that works best: telling and retelling their story. When you can talk about your loss in the presence of others, you can sort out your feelings." (Wright, H. Norman, <u>Experiencing grief</u>, B & H Publishing: Nashville, Tennessee, 2004, p.59)

I guess one thing I came to realize through Bob's death is that grief is not necessarily reliant on love. I say that grief is the price we pay for human connection, whatever that connection may look like. The road for me with Bob in my life in some ways was long. It stretched from sixteen years old to sixty-five years old, both together and apart. Yet, judging from my grief, we were not "apart" enough.

Another article from Mindful Christianity Today said:

> "I had my own notion of grief. I thought it was the sad time that followed the death of someone you love. And you had to push through it to get to the other side. But I'm learning there is no other side. There is no pushing through. But rather, there is absorption. Adjustment. Acceptance. And grief is not something you complete, but rather, you endure. Grief is not a task to finish and move on, but an element of yourself—an alteration of your being, a new way of seeing. A new definition of self." (Author unknown, Facebook, Mindful Christianity Today, April 30, 2020)

I think this applies whether or not you love the person deeply in the present or not. I had to push through whatever feelings I experienced following Bob's death. And I would be lying if I said I had no feelings, that his death did not affect me at all. I think that, even if I had not gotten tied into his last weeks of life, I would still have felt something surrounding his death.

Some former spouses say they have experienced or would experience joy. I can honestly say that I felt no joy, maybe because I am the person that I am. I view human life reverently. Maybe I felt no joy because I was still tied up in Bob's life over the years we were divorced, and, yes, at times aggravated by his behavior or short-sightedness. For me, death is a very somber observance. Death is holy. If a person observes that death, it cannot help but move the observer in some way, perhaps because it is the moment when heaven touches earth. I am a different person today because of Bob's life and because of Bob's death. I feel that I am a better person. Hopefully, that is so.

H. Norman Wright described grief quite accurately. He wrote,

"Your feelings will come and go often for some unknown reason. At other times they will erupt because of some triggers that activated them. . . Going to certain stores, restaurants, or even driving on a certain street can bring back the loss and sadness. These are triggers, and often they are sights, sounds, and even smells. Understanding which ones trigger pleasant or unpleasant memories and emotions can help you know what to move toward and what to move away from during this journey." (Wright, H. Norman, Experiencing Grief, B & H Publishing Group: Nashville, Tennessee, 2004, p.31)

Nicole Gabert wrote,

"Grief, after the initial shock of loss, comes on in waves . . . When you're driving alone in your car, while you're doing the dishes, while you're getting ready for work . . . and all of a sudden it hits you – how so very MUCH you miss someone, and your breath catches, and your tears flow, and the sadness is so great that it's physically painful." (Gabert, Nicole, Facebook, lessonslearnedinlife.com, Mindful Christianity Today, April 17, 2019)

I did feel a strange sadness when triggered by things I saw in my environment. There was a gold, HHR Chevrolet parked along one street near me exactly like the one Bob had driven until the time of his death. Along another street, there was a 4 X 4 Chevrolet Silverado pickup with the same gray and red coloring as the one Bob and I had purchased in 1992. Because Bob had driven a school bus, when school buses drove around my area of the city, I thought of him. Every time I passed a nearby street with the name of Grange Avenue, I thought of the way Bob had called it "Orange" Avenue the last time he drove up to my condo on that Labor Day weekend when hell broke loose at Amy's cabin. It reminded me of how I had encouraged him to get his eyes checked and purchase some decent glasses. I rarely think about Bob these days when I observe these reminders. If I do happen to think of him, there is no sadness.

Power of Positivity posted a writing on grief by Elizabeth I. It reads: "Grief never ends . . . But it changes. It's a passage, not a place to stay. Grief is not a sign of weakness, nor a lack of faith . . . It is the price of love." (Elizabeth I, Facebook, May 23, 2020)

Because I had loved Bob for a long time, I was affected by his death. I experienced and continue to experience grief in some form because of it. But the grief has not been deep sadness. It has been a sense of deep reverence for being the person with whom he chose to take his final journey. I am convinced that grief work is the work of a very strong person. And that faith helps one make that grief journey. And, although, if we never love we might never have to experience grief, also, if we never love, what is life worth? A life without love is empty.

Journaling in a time of grief can be very helpful. My journaling following Bob's unexpected death helped me express my grief thoughts. In July following Bob's death, I wrote:

"Today I am remembering. We begin to remember at such a young age. My four-year-old granddaughter says to me, 'Grandma, remember when . . .' My seven-year-old grandson pulls out a toy I brought back from Bob's house the weekend of the funeral, the weekend with my girls and their husbands cleaning out the farmhouse. He says, 'It smells like Grandpa Bob's house.'

I respond, 'You remember what Grandpa Bob's house smelled like?'

He responds, 'Yes, this doll sure smells like his house. This one too,' as he hands me another doll.

How can a seven-year-old remember such a thing—the smell of must, and mold, and dust that had permeated everything in the old farmhouse where Bob lived. " (June 15, 2018)

We remember with all our senses. That is the beauty, and that is the difficulty—and that is why we grieve. I continued:

"These days I see and smell and feel the memories if I look inward at everything that happened between Bob and me at that house over more than two decades of my life. It is like a video playing in my mind if I so let it. And, sometimes, when I can't help myself, or absent-mindedly, I do let it. As I write this, I begin to feel like my whole body is hurting. I go to the cupboard, retrieve a few aspirin, and take them. I'm not sure aspirin is what I need for this 'hurt' I'm feeling—the hurt so deep inside. I have the air-conditioning going. It is humid today—even for July—but not really all that hot. I notice my arms get goosebumps. I should turn off the air-conditioning. And, yet, if I do, I feel like I might suffocate on all of this—on all these memories. I might drown in this grief." (July 12, 2018)

It was helping me a great deal to journal my grief and to put my thoughts down in writing. On July 22, 2018, I wrote:

"Today is exactly ten months since Bob died. Ten months! We've moved through almost a year of seasons with him gone. It's hard to imagine how fast for me the time has gone.

I still see him at times sitting in the recliner in my condo. I think of something he should take back with him to the farm. Then it jolts into my head—he is gone. He isn't around to do that anymore. I must get rid of things I no longer want in some way myself."

And again:

"When I drive through the streets of the city, I see something I would like to show him—to teach him. And then I think he doesn't need to learn, he has no need to see because neither matter any longer. The simple life he had on our farm is all he ever needed to know." (July 23, 2018)

I wrote on July 25, 2018:

"There will not be those things that go with aging for Bob—eyeglasses, root canals or dentures, really graying hair, using a walker or a wheelchair—all those incapacities of aging will never be part of life for him. In some ways, his early death simplified things for him. In some ways, since he needed so much help, it simplified things for **us**!"

And I continued later:

"There is no sadness now. That 'phase' has passed. Now I contemplate what his death means for me, for my family, for my grandchildren. There is a sense of stillness—silence. But no longer sadness. At least that phase has passed. I have a plaster angel given by a business in Arlington at his funeral. She sits in my porch. She is not sad either. She is serene. She makes me feel serene. Still, silent, and serene describe me now, ten months following his death. That is all." (August 3, 2018)

Some of my thoughts at the time were an assessment of what was, and they were quite profound. One day I wrote:

"Bob would have enjoyed the day today. It is mid-summer with the high temperature in the low 80's—and with low humidity. He could have opened the farmhouse windows and doors and blown away some of that musty smell that has accumulated since I left. He would have been out walking on the farmland, picking up rocks here and there, pulling weeds that weren't discouraged by the weed treatment the renter of the farmland had applied. He would have checked the drain tile intakes and the openings into the ditch to see how much water was running through them. He would maybe have found a dead racoon or opossum, or worse yet, a skunk that somehow met its misfortune. He would have come back to the farmyard energized—a typical farmer in love with his life and his land. That was always him. They say farming is in a farmer's blood. That is for sure. That was Bob. He breathed it in every breath he took—until he no longer took any more breaths, when the autumn sun closed along with the dirt over his farming body. I never really understood it, never 'got it.' I needed more, something different, something more reliable. But for him, the farm was ever and always enough." (July 28, 2018)

In early August of 2018, I was contemplating Bob's behavior during our marriage, which had been so cruel, and if he had any thoughts about that as he was facing what would likely be his death:

"The morning after you slept on my couch, you complimented me on how comfortable the couch was and how well you had slept. You'd slept there occasionally a number of times through the years without ever so much as a word. But that morning, positive words were there. But never was there an admission from you of your extremely abusive behavior which I'd lived with for over two decades. Never was there an 'I'm sorry.' Can I forgive without those two necessities? I'm not superhuman. I wonder what kind of conversation you had those last days and nights with God. Did you go to your grave bearing your guilt? Or did you go with a newly found and received forgiveness? God—and you—only know." (August 2, 2018)

All of my journaling says I was experiencing grief. Even though whatever sadness that I had experienced in the months immediately following his death had passed, I was still moving back and forth between the various aspects of grieving. None of us are immune if we experience a loss. If we are connected in any way to another person, or even to a job, or possession, we will grieve. Grieving is part of being human. It is hard, but I believe we move to greater understanding of ourselves in the grieving process. As a person of faith, I believe we also move to a greater understanding of God.

When I was serving in the parish, and members of my congregations were experiencing loss and grief, I would encourage them to come to church. Often, they would say, "But I know I will cry."

"Yes, you will probably cry. But that will be just fine. Cry through the hymns. Cry through the Bible passages. Cry through the sermon. The tears will be tears of healing, and they must come out in order for you to get through this. No one will mind. They know of your loss. Crying the tears in the context of worship is healthy," I would advise.

I truly believe that the experience of worship is helpful when one is grieving. This belief stems from my own experience. Following my father's death, I cried during the hymns, during the prayers, even as I was in the chancel helping lead the service. I always felt relieved and better afterwards. Being in the church with one's brothers and sisters in Christ—I can't think of a better place to grieve!

CHAPTER **12**

Grace Upon Grace

WE OFTEN REFER to mercy and grace as one and the same action. Though it may seem slight, there is a difference between mercy and grace, which needs to be made clear as we enter a conversation about my interactions with Bob that last month of his life. Reverend Ryan Todt, Wynnbrook Christian School, clarifies this difference. He writes that "mercy is the withholding of punishment. Grace is much larger. It is not just withholding what is bad (punishment), that which is deserved, but also, going beyond that to give a thing that is not deserved." (Todt, Ryan, quora.com, Oct 9, 2018)

To give grace to someone is to give them, not only mercy, but also underserved kindness, and love. That would fit with what I showed Bob by helping him those last weeks of his life. For me, it was an act of grace.

When we think of God's grace towards us, we see that Jesus gave his life for us for our redemption even though we continue to sin and do not deserve it. God has continued to love us even though we often have turned away from God and not shown love for God. Thus, grace is giving something to a person even though that person has done nothing to deserve it. It may include providing something for a person when that person needs it, even though that person has not done something for you when you needed it. Matthew Wong says grace "is going out of your way to bestow your compassion and love towards a person even if they might not appreciate it or return the favor . . . it is choosing to act positively toward someone who might have done you wrong . . . Grace is a totally gratuitous gift." (Wong, Matthew, quora. com, August 4, 2019)

Reverend Frederick Buechner, Theologian, grasps the very human and, also, very Godly elements of grace:

> "Grace is something you can never get but only be given. There's no way to earn it or deserve it or bring it about more than you can deserve the taste of raspberries or ice cream or earn good looks or bring about your own birth. . . A good sleep is grace and so are good dreams. Most tears are grace. The smell of rain is grace. Somebody loving you is grace. You loving somebody is grace. . . The grace of God means something like: Here is your life. You might never have been, but you are because the party wouldn't have been complete with you. Here is this world, beautiful and terrible things will happen. Don't be afraid. I am with you. Nothing can ever separate us. It's for you I created the universe. I love you." (Buechner, Frederick, Wishful Thinking: A Theological ABC, HarperCollins: New York, 1993, pp.33-34)

Grace is a kindness or a favor that is unmerited. It is a free gift with no strings attached. For those of us, who are human, it is perhaps the hardest act we will ever undertake.

Others have told me that what I did for Bob that last month of his life was a gift of grace. These people, some who were friends, some who were former parish members who knew my story, and a therapist agreed. I went to pick up Bob, not one time, but two, without expecting even reimbursement for my time and my gas. Although I wasn't constantly with him in the hospital, I was there at important times. I had preserved his relationship with his daughters, so they also were there for him. I provided much that was required to present him with the funeral and burial he desired. I helped with final, necessary paperwork to provide services and to help get the estate settled. I was not and am not superhuman. I just did what needed to be done at the time. He did not seem to have anyone else close to him, who could do what was needed. It was a gift of grace.

I think several factors went into my behavior at the time. Most importantly, I was raised as a Christian. A Christian provides Christian charity even when it is not easy. A Christian is to show love even when love is not returned. That was the example modeled by my parents, by my Sunday School teachers, and by my pastors. That was the example set by the families our family associated with as my sisters and I grew up.

I also had served as a teacher and program coordinator for mentally and physically disabled children and adults for twenty-one years of my professional life before I went into ministry. It was a continued practice of helping those, who could give very little back. It was loving those that many in the world wish to avoid. I was not above doing the most mundane tasks, even of servicing special, physical needs which my students had.

In a way, also I saw Bob for his mental disabilities. He had high anxiety. He was narcissistic, he had a borderline personality. The attitude I had towards my students I also was able to extend to him—to extend him a lot of grace for behavioral infractions.

Truth Inside You, posted on Facebook on February 14, 2020, reads, "When you finally learn that a person's behavior has more to do with their internal struggle than it ever did with you . . . you learn grace." (Author unknown, Facebook, Truth Inside You, February 14, 2020)

I do not think Bob's behavior was about me. I believe it was an inappropriate way of dealing with high anxiety. I believe it was an aspect of his borderline personality disorder. It may have been an extension of his narcissism. Although he loved farming, I do not think he was emotionally suited to being totally responsible for all that farming entails. The girls and I added more stress to those responsibilities.

He did not handle his stress appropriately. He did not seek help to learn to deal with his stress in more effective ways without harming another person. But realizing why he behaved the way he did, does not excuse his behavior. He went to his grave owning what he had done—unless he had cleared it with God. With my help, he was able to function fairly stably out in society. Perhaps my helping him in the end was simply an extension of how I had helped him when I had been married to him. Primarily, I just did what needed to be done. I did not think at the time that I was going above and beyond the line of duty. I was serving another human being, who was in need of my help, the same as I have done many times while serving in ministry.

I don't think I am alone in this. A woman in my congregation moved down to Florida to help her ex-husband as he was dying. Another woman I know told me that she would help her estranged husband, who was needing heart surgery. At the time I thought these responses were rather strange. But, when the time came, I did the same. Perhaps it is not so strange. Perhaps it is a "woman" thing—that we are capable of putting aside the hurt that was caused or endured to care for a person, who had held major importance in our lives at some point in time.

When I was leaving Bob's hospital room after he had had that first test to check his arteries, to get my car in order to take him home to my condo, I overheard the attending nurse say to Bob, "Your ex-wife is really nice."

He responded, "She is always nice."

Now, I can assure you that I am not always nice. I experience all the same emotions as anyone else, including anger. I make huge blunders at times. I am, however, a caring person. And, at the time Bob needed me, I was able to put the past aside to do for him what needed to be done in the end. Was I an example of God's command to love above all else? Perhaps caring for a person, who does not deserve it, is the truest test of following that command. Then again, perhaps it just happens because, at the time, we are put into a situation in which we just do what is needed at that moment because someone needs us to do it. Perhaps it is just part of being human.

Stan Lee wrote, "That person who helps others simply because it should or must be done, and because it is the right thing to do, is indeed without a doubt, a real superhero." (Lee, Stan, Facebook, Mindful Christianity Today, May 21, 2019). I would not call myself a superhero. I just did what I did for Bob in the end. He was another human being. Because of that, I could show care for him.

All my thoughts on grace were tested this last year. I had been suffering from low hemoglobin since 2013. Doctors ran all kinds of tests, but everything came back negative.

I was bleeding internally, but we could not figure out from where. Finally, last summer, a surgeon ordered an esophagram x-ray. The cause finally showed up. Part of my stomach was lying on top of my diaphragm. On top of it, a hernia had developed with a Camron lesion. The lesion was bleeding.

During one test, I asked the attending nurse how part of a person's stomach could be on top of a one's diaphragm. She said usually it happens in one of two ways. A multiple birth pregnancy could cause enough force to push the stomach up. Or else, an accident in which a person receives a hard blow to the stomach area could do it. My heart sank. My legs felt week. At some point, one of Bob's blows or kicks to my stomach had pushed part of the stomach above the diaphragm. The hernia probably had been there for a while. Trouble came when the Camron lesion developed. After what I learned and what I went through this past winter, I decided that sometimes grace is heavy. Sometimes it is the hardest thing to give because it is totally undeserved. I journaled on January 13, 2020, "Tomorrow is surgery to put the stomach back in place—the stomach Bob punched and kicked out of place. Which time is the sad question? There were so many times, I have no idea 'which time' it occurred. Tonight, grace is very, very heavy."

My stomach was probably on top of my diaphragm for a long time, for years. It was not until I became older, developed the hernia, and then the lesion, that the low hemoglobin became an ongoing issue requiring continual blood and iron infusions.

After surgery in January and one last set of iron infusions in February, I am healthy again. It took seven years to get here. This summer I have energy again, and it is wonderful.

Perhaps my ability to be able to extend grace to Bob when needed was not rooted in me at all. Perhaps it was simply God working through me. As a Christian, the difficulties in my life have been defined by God's presence in my life.

When I was in my abusive marriage and in the difficulties of trying to eek out a living on the farm, I leaned heavily on the Psalms to see me through the extremely difficult times. The words of Psalm 46 were often in my mind as our crops would be destroyed by storms, or the cattle suffered illness, as I knew another beating would take place. "The LORD is my refuge and strength, a very present help in trouble," would be my prayer as I put on my chores clothes and set out in the torrents of rain to find my swearing husband and try to help with the situation that was angering him. I knew that often I would be at a loss to control the situation or the beating that would follow. But God was always with me in my suffering. I relinquished my desire for control to God. In doing so, I experienced God's grace, which transcended the situation at hand, and gave me hope for the future and brighter days to follow.

Jerry Sittser states it in this way;

"But in coming to the end of ourselves, we can also come to the beginning of a vital relationship with God. Our failures can lead us to grace and to a profound spiritual awakening. . . we reach the point where we begin to search for a new life, one that depends less on circumstances and more on the depth of our souls. . . We feel the need for something beyond ourselves, and it begins to dawn on us that reality may be more than we once thought it to be. We begin to perceive hints of the divine, and our longing grows. To our shock and bewilderment, we discover that there is a Being in the universe who, despite our brokenness and sin, loves us fiercely. In coming to the end of ourselves, we have come to the beginning of our true and deepest selves. We have found the One, whose love gives shape to our being." (Sittser, Gerald, A Grace Disguised, Zondervan: Grand Rapids, Michigan, 2004, p. 90)

It is when we realize that we are not in control and can never be fully in control regardless of how dependent on ourselves we think we are or wish to be, that we come to know what grace truly is. And in the experiencing of grace from a God, whose love for us knows no bounds, we can act with grace, serve with grace, and extend grace even when it seems to someone on the outside that it would be impossible. I live with God's grace daily. Grace informs and leads my life, even when it demands more than it would seem I can realistically give. That is the gift of which my involvement in Bob's death and the physical and spiritual processing of all that followed has made me vitally aware.

Grace is, in the end, all anyone can ask of us. Pure and simple. We care because we know what it is like to hurt, or suffer, or be alone. That is the teaching of Jesus. That is the teaching I expound as a pastor. Can I not personally follow my own teaching? Kindness is always a choice. Mercy is perhaps not big enough for this situation. Grace, therefore, becomes the defining action. Or maybe grace leads to mercy and kindness and is inseparable from them. Either way, there is grace. And grace is big. Very, very big. And grace is, as the hymn says, quite amazing.

CHAPTER 13

Moving Forward

WHAT WERE THE days and weeks like for me and for my family following Bob's unexpected death? How was life different even though Bob had not been a frequent part of our lives for a long time?

In the weeks immediately following Bob's death, I needed quiet time. I wanted to be alone to process the death, the funeral, and cleaning up the farm. In my mind, I could watch all of it as if a video were playing in my mind. It all moved me deeply even though I was not Bob's loving spouse. I wrote, "I can't begin to imagine how hard and how much it hurts to lose a loving spouse with whom one is living."

Probably one of the reasons my feelings were intense was that I could still vividly remember how we had worked together on the farm. We were not a couple in which both spouses went their separate ways to work and who spent leisurely evenings together. Although I taught during the day, Bob and I worked together with the cattle and with the crops in nearly every other waking hour that we were together. I journaled:

> "We learned to be synchronized. Where I gave the brain power, Bob contributed the strength. We got many jobs done—together. Perhaps working together like that created some kind of bond between us, a bond that even divorce

couldn't nullify. But in death, that bond was also torn apart. For me, there was no love left. The love had grown tired of giving—like to a child who couldn't or wouldn't grow up." (July 28, 2018)

Krista, on the other hand, felt the need to be with me more than ever. She definitely was shaken in a way that pushed her to be close. I tolerated that as much as I could, but because I, too, had to process everything, I could not talk through everything with her as she would have liked.

Krista also brought her six-year-olds with her. I love my grandchildren, but the commotion of children when a person is grieving is very difficult. Even Amy, who was at home with her three, ages six, three, and one, attested to that.

Shortly after Bob's death and burial, one of Krista's twins went out into my porch while here. Again, he quickly came back into the living room, saying, "Grandpa is here. Grandpa is here."

Krista and I were confused. Then, he added, "I can smell him." It is amazing the triggers that make a person identifiable! The odor of Bob's clothing, which I had not yet donated, still hung in the confines of the porch.

As Lars and my girls worked at settling the estate, by December, they were taking steps to sell the farm and putting out bids. By late January, the buyer and the girls closed on the farm sale. Later that winter, we learned the buyer was in the process of selling the farm place to another buyer. All the details of the estate, over time, were dealt with. The farm, although always a part of my families' past, was, now, not part of our family's future going forward.

We celebrated the first Christmas after Bob's death in the party room of my condo. We ate the chili, which I had made, along with various treats the girls had brought. We opened gifts, always an exciting time with the grandchildren. This was followed by swimming in the building's pool. The girls and their husbands had some details of the estate to take care of, which they did while they were together. They mentioned Bob's absence, mainly that he wasn't there "talking constantly." The grandchildren made no mention of him.

In April, I received an invitation from Abbott-Northwestern Hospital to attend a recognition ceremony for the donation of Bob's corneas. Although I knew that someone today has better sight because of Bob's death—that good purpose resulting from his death, not being his wife, I did not feel it was my place to attend. I asked the girls if any of them wanted to go. None did. Bob had burned his bridges. The hurt he had caused them permeated their connection to him. So, no one was at the ceremony to represent his gift of sight to someone in need.

Later, I received a certificate in a nice, leather-like folder, commemorating the cornea donation. I asked the girls if anyone wanted the certificate. Again, no one spoke up. I kept it at my condo for a few weeks. But on one fine May day the following spring, I dropped it in my waste basket, along with the funeral folder and memorial cards, which had sat in the dish tub under my coffee table since Bob's death. It all went out with the trash.

What happens when someone so badly hurts those, with whom he is supposed to be in a loving relationship, that the caring connection is lost? In the end, no one really cares. Our daughters, although affected by his death, have not been mourning him with sadness. They are noticing his absence—sometimes.

In May following Bob's death, I began the process of procuring a gravestone for him. Since the girls were busy with jobs and families in three different states, the task fell to me. With only a little input from my daughters, I ordered a simple, gray stone with his name and birth and death dates. At my oldest daughter's request, I had a sprig of wheat placed near the top by the last name "Dahlke." The proof for the stone arrived on exactly the one-year anniversary of his death. The stone would take until the following spring to be completed and set up on the cemetery. Now his grave would not be anonymous.

The summer following Bob's death, the condo building where I live was putting a new, retaining wall on the downward slope between the back of the building and the lake behind it. Part of the project required a skid-steer loader to travel back and forth from the parking lot to the area behind the building where the retaining wall was being built. Having the engine of the skid-steer loader scraping, loading, and the sound of it trailing off behind the building again, took me back to the many hours I had spent on our skid-steer loader on the farm scraping the cattle's feel lot, scooping sileage to put in the feed bunk, and hauling bales from the machine shed. The roar, as the skid-steer loader came around my condo building and trailed back again to where it had come from, was the same sound I was so familiar with on the farm. Just these little occurrences stirred my memories that first year following his death.

In July, I noted what would have been Bob's and my forty-fourth wedding anniversary had we still been married, the forty-ninth year since we had begun dating—not quite a half century. I wrote, "It is little wonder I have some lingering feelings about his death not withstanding rides up to the cabin, to birthday parties, and to the weddings of our girls. He helped me move just one year ago, carrying heavy boxes out of my apartment to vehicles for me—with a 'ripe' brain tumor waiting to wreak havoc with his life, and, thus, also with mine." (July 13, 2018)

That summer, our family would receive exciting news. A new grandchild was on the way. Amy was pregnant. This grandchild, who would never know his grandfather except perhaps through conversation and pictures, was to be born in late January. He would join the brood of five grandchildren, who were already very much a part of my life. Maggie, who was now talking fluently, was excited to share the news.

"Where is the baby?" I asked her.

"Here in mommy's belly," she responded happily pointing to Amy's abdomen.

Baby Warren Richard, named after my father and Lars' godfather, was born on January 25, 2019.

I went to Amy and Lars' cabin over the Fourth of July that summer. It was my first trip to the cabin following Bob's death although I had driven there by myself many times before. During the time that I was there, Lars and Will, Amy and Lars' oldest son, were out on the lake in the boat fishing. Ordinarily, Bob would have gone out with them. I thought of how peaceful it must be for them to fish without having to listen to and entertain Bob, keeping him out of Amy's hair—out of all of our hair. Yet, I wrote,

> "It is the Fourth of July week, ten months since the night Bob breathed his last. We've moved from fall to winter to spring to summer. Yet, he looms heavy in the air. I've not been back to the grave since mid-November. Once in a while I feel the urge to stand there, to feel the rural, prairie wind blow over the growing corn. I want to see what the farm's new buyer has planted, to see if anything on the farmyard has changed. I wonder about that strange butterfly that, all alone, at the grave site, seemed to have a message meant just for me as it fluttered from my elbow, along the casket, and into the trees—making a determined path." (July 4, 2018)

On the first anniversary of Bob's death, the girls and their families gathered at my condo building. After having a fun afternoon swimming in the pool, they came up to my apartment for pizza. The mood of the day was festive and joyful. It had been a tough and busy year. Many major decisions had been made. Much work had been done. We had all survived it—happy and connected.

As I said before, during the first two—and more—years following Bob's death, the PTSD dreams increased and continued. The dreams seemed to persist with a vengeance. On May 12, 2019, I journaled,

"In my dream I'm picking up empty sacks from seed and feed, and all the strings which had bound those paper sacks. Bob has left them lying everywhere around the farmyard, in the machine shed, and in the garage. I have two fires going to consume them. I stop to feel which way the wind is blowing to know where it is safe to light the fires. Company is coming for a birthday party. Some have already arrived and are visiting in the house. I am anxious to get to the house, but I have to clean up the mess Bob left all over first. Some of his friends are helping. All of a sudden there is a rush of water. A drinking cup is running over in the barn. Bob hollers at me that I have not kept that under control. What a mess! Now there are metal pieces also mixed between the paper sacks. The mess never ends. Bob's yelling never ends. I wake up. Relief!"

Of another dream, I wrote again,

"I am walking around the farmyard picking of oily, farm-dirty clothing—work jeans, sweatshirts, jackets. I'm trying to get them all washed within a short period of time or else a beating will follow. They are found on the ground saturated with mud, on the floors of tractor seats, in tractor cabs, under hay and straw. I keep adding to the wash already agitating in the tub. I am trying to avoid Bob's anger, but his yelling makes me believe that it will not end without a beating." (May 20, 2019)

Bob always left his work clothes wherever he took it off. It would gradually get covered with mud, oil, hay or straw, and dirt and dust.

He would then get angry when these items would have to be replaced and the money that I would have to spend to replace them. Even after his death, when I walked through the machine shed, his good, red, down, winter jacket lay between the dirt and dust in the shed. It has taken until the last couple of months, over two years following his death, for the dreams to begin to subside. I hope that continues.

In May of 2019, baby Warren was baptized. Because Bob had always accompanied me on the occasions of baptism for our other five grandchildren, I noticed his absence. I was not upset or grieving over it, but I did notice it. I was alone making the hour-long drive to Wisconsin where Amy and Lars live. I was alone waiting in the car and, later, in the church until the rest of my family arrived and I could join them in the reserved pews. I was acutely aware of that as Lars' parents entered the church together. The cold, rainy, spring day seemed to be saying something about his absence.

Time has a way of changing things, especially when it comes to children. Several months after his baptism, Warren was rolling, sitting, reaching, teething, smiling, and laughing. He is now running and learning to talk. He is the grandchild that Bob will never know. Maggie, eighteen months at the time of Bob's death, will be starting pre-Kindergarten. She has changed so much. She's become so outgoing, and she talks constantly. The other grandchildren have grown such long legs, and they are smart as whips.

Bob said he wanted to see his grandsons grow up. They have been steadily and quickly growing. They are now finishing second and third grade—so much more knowledgeable than almost three years ago. And Bob is not being given the privilege of seeing them. A person might think that the fact that he is not seeing them grow is a fitting punishment for his behavior. I do not feel that way. I do not think God punishes that way. The fact that Bob is not here just is. It just is. I am not God, and that is not my determination to make.

I grew up without knowing one of my grandfathers. My dad's

father had passed away eight years before I was born. Although, when I was young, I rarely thought about that fact, as I have gotten older, I have wondered about him. What did he look like? What was he like as a person? What was he interested in? What was his life like raising a family through the depression and World War II? My grandmother spoke very little of him. And I never saw a picture of him until two years ago. Even then, he had on a hat with a wide brim, so he was hard to see.

Warren will have pictures. Warren will come to know Bob through our memories. Hopefully, the good memories will be passed on to a greater degree than the abusive ones. He will know of what his grandfather died. And what he might look for in himself.

The two-year anniversary of Bob's death did not pass without my noting it. I thought of the gravestone, which I had seen for the first time in person at the end of May—so solid, gray, and cold. It fits Bob, always a solid worker, a simple person with no frills about him, but without empathy and decency for those closest to him. Why would I go out of my way to help him? Simply because I was asked. Simply because of grace—grace, which is both immensely complicated and also, at the same time, pure and simple.

CHAPTER **14**

New Dimensions

IN OCTOBER OF 2019 on a beautiful, warm day, twenty-five months after Bob's death, Krista, I, and Krista's twins, headed out to the cemetery where Bob was buried and then, to the farm. I had seen the stone soon after it was placed in the spring, shortly before Memorial Day. But none of the girls had seen it.

It was sunny that day, but it was also very windy. The cemetery grass, which by late October had grown to several inches tall, blew like shallow waves in the gusty, prairie wind. By mid-afternoon, the sun had begun to descend behind the evergreens on the west side of the cemetery casting the row of stones in which Bob's stone rests in partial shade.

As Krista, I, and the boys climbed out of her van, the boys quickly ran to where they remembered his casket had sat over two years earlier. They could read now, so reading the stone, they announced that they were in the right place. We soon joined them. Then we gave them the task of searching out other stones with the same name "Dahlke."

Krista and I walked quietly, pushing against the windy gusts so familiar in this area of the state. Krista was seeking some closure that had been evading her. She was also curious how the stone looked. I wanted to see and feel whatever came to mind these many months after the whole ordeal of his death and funeral.

As I walked, I felt a presence or "presences" enclosed in this sacred space. If there were spirits, they were peaceful and welcoming of our being there. The peacefulness I felt was the same feeling I had experienced that late September day two years earlier as we committed Bob's body to the ground. There was a comforting presence and a comforting peace.

We slowly perused the rows of stones, pointing out relatives to the boys, who had been buried there. At one point, Krista asked how I felt seeing the stone and the grave. I admitted that I had mixed feelings. Bob was my husband of almost twenty-four years. We had worked hard together. We had shared the good with the bad. Yet, his abuse was a common theme throughout that time and the reason that I finally left. Over time, however, we had maintained some connection as he wanted to be involved in our daughters' and grandchildren's lives. He had called on me to help him in the end. I responded with grace, a decision that has affected the last two plus years. But to this day, I do not in any way regret the actions that I took. Forgiveness is a very powerful thing. It doesn't take away the natural consequences of one's actions. But it does leave room for healing. It does leave room for grace. God is good, indeed, very good.

After our time at the cemetery, we travelled less than a mile to the farm where Bob lived and where we had farmed together. The land, sold and run by another farmer, stood from end to end and side to side with ripened corn. The row of trees that had run the full length of the ditch bank, within which the water flowed diagonally through the farm, was completely gone. There was just an open expanse of corn between the cemetery and the farm.

I noticed a number of changes on the farmyard itself. The couple, who had bought the farmyard, had done much work to clean it up. A new well stood in the middle of the yard. A mound system for sewage lay across the length where the granary had been. The old, calf barn, that was left in rubble following the fire in 1997, was gone. The lean behind the barn, which had collapsed from the weight of snow a number of years ago, had been repaired. Horses were grazing out of the machine shed. Puppies were being raised in the garage. The trees, which had shaped the east lawn, were gone. Badly needed gravel had been hauled.

The house also had many changes. Among them were new windows, new shingles, new siding, and a new addition. The big, white farmhouse was now brown. There was a beautiful front door with an etched glass design in the window. The white shingles had been replaced with black ones. Where there had been two doors, there was now only one. So, it now looked very different on the outside.

The inside also was in the process of being remodeled. Sometimes, as one of the new owners showed us through it, it would look very different. And I would have trouble getting my bearings. Then I would come around a corner, and there would be something so familiar, I would be taken aback. Then I knew that I was back in the house of my married life. The built-in, china cupboard was there. The arch between the dining room and living room with the pocket doors was there. The old, basement door had not been changed. A piano I bought from another family on Bob's and my tenth anniversary was there although it now stood in the dining room instead of the living room. The carved, wooden design on the front of the piano looked so rich with the sun shining through the new patio door, which had replaced the old, bay window. Many rooms were painted in bright colors and decorated with special paintings and sayings. It was very welcoming. I had the distinct feeling that, even though I thought this house would be destroyed, it was, in actuality, being resurrected. New life had risen out of death. What once was dead now was living once again filled with family—children and lots of love!

I was struck by the strong feeling of resurrection that I was witnessing. That is the way it is with God I have discovered in my now sixty-eight years of living. There is a never-ending saga of life, death, and new life on this earth. Perhaps it is the breaking in in increments of what will be the ultimate reality of the world to come. I am so peaceful these days. So incredibly peaceful as I journey. Oh, how God walks with me!

The most striking aspect of Bob's death for me, and, I guess, of death itself, was and is its total silence. All the words Bob had, all the noise of it, is completely gone. His silence is as hard and cold as the stone marking his grave. Death, when it comes, delivers a total silence we are not accustomed to in our lives in which sound and noise of some type fill almost every moment. I became intensely aware of this when Krista and I visited the cemetery last fall.

If we were not speaking, the only thing to be heard was the wind. Just silence—so final in its emptiness! Silence, pure and simple.

The second most striking aspect for me was the "holiness" of it. It was almost as if I, and Amy and Lars, as the observers in Bob's ICU room the night he died, could see and feel another dimension entering and surrounding the room. This was partly due to the reverence with which the hospital staff treated Bob. Carefully, the IV needles were removed, and the cover was straightened around his body. The staff worked quietly and diligently.

The next summer, I was watching a video on the embalming process. It stressed the extreme respect given to the body as it is prepared for the reviewal. The mortician, who was showing the process and speaking her way through the steps she takes, stated that she treats every cadaver as if it is a member and loved one in her family because every body she prepares is a member of someone's family. That kind of holiness, she said, was the least she could do at a time when family and friends are grieving.

After two weeks had passed following Bob's burial, and I stood at the edge of his grave, the outline of the rectangle that had been dug to accommodate the vault was still a clear line. As I have noted, on top of the black soil, which had filled in the open grave, grass seed had been tossed. Because the weather had been cloudy and wet, some of the grass had sprouted. There were spindles in a haphazard pattern on top of the grave. By the time I saw the grave over two years later, the soil and the grass blended smoothly into the carpet of grass covering the entire cemetery between the stones.

Maybe that is how we also heal from grief. Gradually, the new life, which we have without the person, grows in and fills the empty and painful spaces that are left early on. Perhaps that growth is symbolized by the passing of the seasons—the cycle of dying and living again that has been orchestrated into creation itself. The green of new life bursts through more and more each day in the springtime until one hardly notices the few death elements left over—a few brown spindles of grass or an occasional dead leaf. That is the way the house and farm are now. Little by little, new life has been bursting forth.

As I write, it is late May. The weather is warm, sunny, and beautiful. My third summer of flowers following Bob's death are blooming outside of my porch door. They are lovely, and I am enjoying them this year more than ever.

We are living through the world novel coronavirus pandemic. I have been under stay-at-home orders for the last three months, so I have not seen my daughters and grandchildren other than through technology since February. Thank goodness for technology, I think! Because of my January surgery and needing to heal from that and regain some immunity, and also, because of my age, now sixty-eight, I am at high risk. There are no medications and is no vaccine to stop the pandemic right now. As of today, nearly two million people in the United States have become infected, and more than 106,000 have died. That puts Bob's death in some perspective. Many are grieving on this day. Many are adjusting to life without a loved one. Some are adjusting to the loss of many of their loved ones.

Since I have been alone during these months, I have had a great deal of time to think about the last almost three years. I have been able to review everything that occurred regarding Bob's death. And I have been able to see how we, his family, have come through it. I think we are stronger, more knowledgeable, and have more wisdom. I think we are more appreciative of the little things in life—peace, laughter, hugs, children's chatter. I think we are more empathetic of the losses of others. Relationships become more important. Death and grief force growth. There is no choice.

On the way home from the hospital in January following my surgery, as Bonnie drove, we crossed the creek near the cluster of condos where I live. As we went over the bridge, I noticed that the bed of ice on the surface of the creek was closing in from its banks on the sides. Soon the creek would be a silent, still plate of glass. It seemed like a wound healing shut.

The grief response to the death of my ex-husband has been like the creek, flowing and ebbing in the breeze. Slowly the grief is healing over just as the ice was overtaking the freedom of the creek's flow. Will the grief open again? Probably as some memory of him arises. Just as the creek opened again this spring, some form of grief may bubble up from where it still festers. But I think any tears I or the girls may have had are healed over. The shock and the trauma hold less power over us. Whatever grief we might still need to experience will be less and less as time passes. Perhaps, with time, that grief will just turn to memories instead.

I think of Bob at times, though not every day as I did soon after the time of his death. I think of what I did for Bob in the end and the choices I and the girls made. Even his gravestone fits him. I am glad that I did what I did at the end of Bob's life. I am glad I did what I needed to do. My actions matched the way I try to live my life. I am reminded each time I am connected to our girls and their families that this is time that I am being given that Bob was not given. This time is my gift from God, who guides my life. There are no cruel, phone calls from him. There is no criticizing. There is no working his needs into our family's events and special times. But I also have some good memories of my time with him. I know now that not everything is all bad. I am living into my future without him with grace.

I think we often feel that death is scary. I compare it to the little maple tree outside my window. One day last fall, it was filled with golden leaves. Then the wind came up. The next day, it was nearly bare. A few, lonely leaves hung on against the gloomy chill. In a way, the tree had died. But, now that it is spring, the green leaves are vibrant once again. The tree has come back to life. Perhaps that is the way death comes into our lives. One day a person is alive. Then, into what seems to happen so quickly at the time, death pushes its way, without announcing itself, it seems, without warning. We need to mourn what was lost and adjust to the new reality. New life continually comes into that new reality if we are open to receiving it.

I have come to believe, having witnessed the deaths of many in my ministry, that dying can be scary, painful, or even very hard. But death can also be very peaceful. Death itself *is* peaceful, and it finally arrives quietly. It is like the wavy, warm breeze on a bright, sunlit, fall day. And the dying person, although gone in the physical body, lives on in the minds and memories of the living. When I look inward instead of outward, I see so many, who have been so dear to me, alive and laughing, being classically themselves. In my mind, they continue to be fully alive. Maybe that is part of the mystery that is death—one of the ways a person continues to live after they die.

Sherri Bessi-Eckert has written:

"You can't give up on love because others are hateful. You can't give up on believing in one another because you've been let down. You can't give up on hope because pain came your way. You can't give up on kindness because some people are cruel. You can't give up on peace because war surrounds you. You can't give up on dreams because they don't always come true. Life isn't about bliss. Life is about learning to live, love, hope, and believe in the midst of perfect imperfection. Life is messy, complicated, confusing, and beautiful all at the same time. Life is the single best gift you have ever been

123

given." (Bessi-Eckert, Sherri, MA, <u>Simple Human</u>, "You Can't Give Up", Facebook, September 21, theothersideofugly.com, Beaverton, Oregon)

I have not given up. The girls and their families have not given up. We move forward in busy, creative, noisy, messy, and inspiring ways. We have grown through Bob's death because we have felt the depth and holiness of it—the profoundness that death brings. We have wisdom we could not have gained in any other way, whether we regard the loss as difficult or freeing. Perhaps it is some of both. And grace, God's grace, has been with us within and, now, beyond that time.

Perhaps we all look at death a little differently because of experiencing the death of someone we have had in our lives, even if we are no longer in a relationship with that person as we might have hoped. Perhaps we understand how quickly death can come. I think we can all appreciate life more because of the experience. Perhaps that is the gift which death gives us. Perhaps that is the grace of it. Death leads to the experience of grace for the survivors if they open their hearts to God. And God's grace leads us to fuller and more abundant life. As I have said before, God is good—very, very good. And, indeed, that is a wonderful thing.

Funeral Sermon

John 14:1-7
"Do not let your hearts be troubled. Believe in God, believe also in me. In my Father's house there are many dwelling places. If it were not so, would I have told you that I go to prepare a place for you? And if I go and prepare a place for you, I will come again and will take you to myself, so that where I am, you may be also. And you know the way to the place where I am going." Thomas said, "Lord, we do not know where you are going. How can we know the way?" Jesus said to him, "I am the way, and the truth, and the life. No one comes to the Father except through me. If you know me, you will know my Father also. From now on you do know him and have seen him."

Grace and peace to you from our loving parent God, from our Lord and Savior, Jesus Christ, and from the Spirit, who gives us life:

Dear Relatives, Friends, Family, Co-workers, and Brothers and Sisters in Christ,
On behalf of my daughters and myself, I would like to thank you for being here today. It has been an unbelievably difficult couple of weeks for all, and the girls are glad of your support today. I also want to thank Pastor Danson for granting me the opportunity to speak to you. Thank you.

Gathering at the time of a death is not only a tradition and ritual, but it is an opportunity to express grief, find some closure in order to reorganize and reframe life, and move forward.

It is also our opportunity to formally commend Bob to God's care and keeping, and to proclaim the redemption and salvation granted to all of us through Jesus Christ our Lord.

Where to start: I remember the rainy, April evening when he first asked me to prom, those early dates, studying together in the library at Morris, our 105 degree wedding day. Like any relationship, it was not all bad and early days were quite good.

Once we returned to the farm, things gradually began to change. I can't explain the mental, social, and behavioral deterioration that occurred first slowly, and, in these later years and weeks, more rapidly. A definite mental deterioration was present, whether by choice or not. He could never bring himself to say he was sorry, to me or to our daughters. I think his giving up on the care of the farm was part of that. And he did try doing things for us, even helping me move in July.

I've heard comments that all of this went really quickly. Well, for me not really. He complained of constant headaches and a stiff neck, eye pressure, and weepy eyes as early as last February. When he rode with me to Ellsworth for Baby Maggie's first birthday at the end of April, he was having endurance and balance issues. I encouraged him that day, as well as numerous times throughout the summer, to seek medical help.

He experienced a severe headache and bleed into his eye socket and from his nose and mouth about a month ago. Three days later, when he was telling me about this, I was like, "You've got to go to the Dr.! This could happen again, and it could be fatal!" He went to emergency where he was diagnosed with sinusitis. When he called me and told me, my response was, "Well, it would be wonderful if that is all it is, but I don't believe it." A **CAT** scan within the week revealed otherwise.

In the meantime, he was driving sports teams and teachers' in-service trips. My fear, that I expressed to him was that, if he didn't seek help, he could take a whole busload of kids down with him. The **CAT** scan set in motion the whole series of events, which has brought us to this day. Life support was removed a week ago Friday, and Bob passed away peacefully at 7:08 p.m.

We all face death, not only with sadness, but also, with some degree of wonder. What is this Kingdom Jesus has prepared for us? Where is it? What will it be like. And what will we be like in it?—**All questions as old as Jesus' death and resurrection I am sure.**

One of my 6-year-old grandsons, Henry, phrased some questions of which our own questions might be only slightly more sophisticated.
   * Is heaven farther away that outer space?
   * If there are no cars in heaven, how do people get around?—then he kind of answered it himself: "Now Grandpa is learning to fly first."
   * Does Grandpa know people in heaven?—Now he is friends with Great-Grandma Lamkie (who also passed this summer).

Jesus said, in God's Kingdom, there are many dwelling places. In some older versions "dwelling places" is translated as "mansions." "In my Father's house, there are many mansions."

In Arlington, there are probably not too many mansions. But in the Twin Cities, there are areas in the city where there are these huge, huge, concrete and brick structures. I've done some weddings in them, and the number of rooms—well, you can get lost in them. Imagine mansions as numerous as the stars—room for Bob, room for you and me someday.

As far as outer space, Henry, all the outer space out there fits into God's realm—all the planets, stars, galaxies, black holes, everything we have discovered, and all that we have no knowledge of as yet.

But I also think God's realm is right here among us in our imperfection today. I believe the perfector is here in this space, invisible to us in our human, earthly state. As we move our arms through the air, we may in some way be touching it, touching God's presence, even as we breathe the Spirit with each breath we take. We cannot fathom the size of God's love or God's care for us after death as well as in this life.

Forgiveness is a hard thing—for us humans that is.
Perhaps Bob was asking for it from me the night before his first surgery when he said, as I was cooking supper, "It really smells good!" As we were eating, he added, "Boy, this chicken is good!" Although he had never complained about my cooking, and had always eaten heartily, out of the hundreds of meals I had prepared for him through time, this was the first compliment. I responded, "Good, it's a rotisserie chicken from Walmart."—too honest, I guess!

A week ago, Monday, when Bob came out of the surgery, which removed the tumor, there were literally 6-8 medical personnel scrambling to take care of various aspects of his immediate care.
Throughout our time together, Bob was always very critical of the girls and I ever getting any medical or dental care, and even prevented it at times. So, as I turned to leave, with my PTSD, I had a flashback of a time I really needed help, and he did everything in his power to prevent me from getting it.

I felt extreme anger in that moment as I left Abbott. Of course, the anger turned to tears, as it always does for me, by the time

I reached my car. When I got home, I texted the girls about this anger. Amy replied that she was wondering what was going on because I had this blank stare on my face.

The following afternoon, as I was lying on my bed, partly in contemplation and partly in prayer, all of a sudden, I heard in my mind Simon Peters' question to Jesus:

"How many times are we to forgive someone who has wronged us, as many as 7x's?"

Jesus replied, "As many as 7x7, or 77 x's, or even 700x700 x's."

We are to forgive again, and again, and again, and again. I knew this, but I had always thought of it in terms of forgiving separate offenses. That day God's message was clear to me: Sometimes we need to forgive the same offense or cluster of offenses over and over and over again. I've learned to trust these Godly messages both through reading of near-death experiences and in the otherworldly interventions in my own life. This extreme peace came over me that afternoon, and it has been present with me all the days since.

Jesus continually taught and modeled God's forgiveness.
Even on the cross, to the repentant criminal, he said,

"Today you will be with me in paradise."

Later, as he hung in mortal pain inflicted on him by the religious and political powers, his words were,

"Father, forgive them, for they know not what they do."

The example of Jesus, even when hanging on the cross, confirms Jesus' teaching and modeling of forgiveness throughout his lifetime. We are to follow his example.

Of course, Jesus' greatest gift to us, won through his death and resurrection, is our redemption, which makes possible our salvation. Baptized with water and the word, signed and sealed with the cross and Holy Spirit, we are all children of God, recipients of this gracious gift.

This gift of salvation was for Bob as well. Forgiveness, redemption, salvation. When God called Bob home last Friday evening, God had a place for Bob among the many mansions in his Kingdom. We wait for the day when we also will join Jesus in the next life that is waiting for us. This was Bob's hope. And this is our hope—and our confidence.

Thanks be to God!
Amen.

September 27, 2017 by Evelyn Dahlke

That I Must Grieve You Twice
(An Abused Wife on the Death of Her Once Spouse)

I grieved you once
after you came down upon me
hard as iron,
again and again and again,
in every way
you knew how to hurt.
For over twenty years
I absorbed your anger,
bore your ill will,
and talked you down.
Then I soothed you,
like a child,
who needed to be reassured,
that you were worthy,
respectable,
loveable,
and most certainly, at least,
okay.
I mothered you,
yet bore your pain
until I broke.
And even then, you were angry,

selfish, and self-absorbed.

Yes, I grieved you once
from the day I left you
until I made for myself
a new life,
a good life,
a free life—without you.
It was hard—so hard
because I left with you
my hopes and dreams
for all that we might have together—
family, intimacy,
shared experiences
and memories,
all those things a young woman
believes about the Cinderella tale.

But you had only room
for **your** dreams,
and how I could help make
those dreams come true.
"What about my dreams?"
I cried at last void of my own personhood,
and I found in you an empty chasm
that had no room for "other."
So, I left
because that was all there was to do.
And I grieved you once,
as one who has lost a lover,
a partner,
who still lives on the earth,
but no longer in the heart.

But must I grieve you twice,
you, who waited with your illness
until I feared you might hurt others?
Then, despite all best efforts
on your behalf,
you died.
You breathed your last
in that hospital bed.
And I was left
to clean up your messes,
doing with our offspring
what you were unable or unwilling
to do yourself.

Must I grieve you twice
as I stare at the finality of your grave
and how the green grass
has already sprouted
above your sleeping head?
You, the powerful, lie powerless
in your eternal rest
as I walk through the memories,
viewing the past like snapshots
flashing through my mind.
As the autumn wind blows
through sun-baked trees,
and your farmyard sleeps
empty,
silent,
untouched by you
in late fall's shortening days,
your weathered machinery,
rusty and worn,
waits to be hauled away.

Can I cry unfair?
So fowl,
so cruel,
that my mind must be stuck
in the emptiness
of your non-being.
I am not even able to exclaim
in the void
my discomfort with a saddening tear.

My grief is an empty grief,
a dry grief,
a stuck-in-my-throat-and-chest kind of grief.
I wear it like a heavy cloak
as the days grow dark
and the clouds hang low
like dampened clothes
left on the line
in the humidness of a late fall night.

I'm afraid that it is so—
that I must grieve you twice
as your permanent absence
weighs as heavily on me
as the freshly turned earth
weighs heavily on you.
Is it because I helped you in the end?
Was able to reach my hands and heart
across the expansive chasm?
Was it that you said some kind words
so completely out of character,
you have left me wondering
what you really meant?

That I let you in enough
so I became involved
in your demise?

You didn't deserve my help
before I left you
nor did you now.
Yet, I allowed you grace enough,
to open a once-closed door
just a sliver
for our lives to intersect.
And because of my gift to you,
though given simply
as one human to another,
I allowed you in.
So, now that you are gone,
what is also true
is that in your absence,
I know for certain
that I must surely grieve you twice.

Evelyn Dahlke
November 16, 2017

Grief Model
(Stroebe & Schut)

The Dual Process Model of Coping with Bereavement
Stroebe & Schut (Death Studies, 1999)

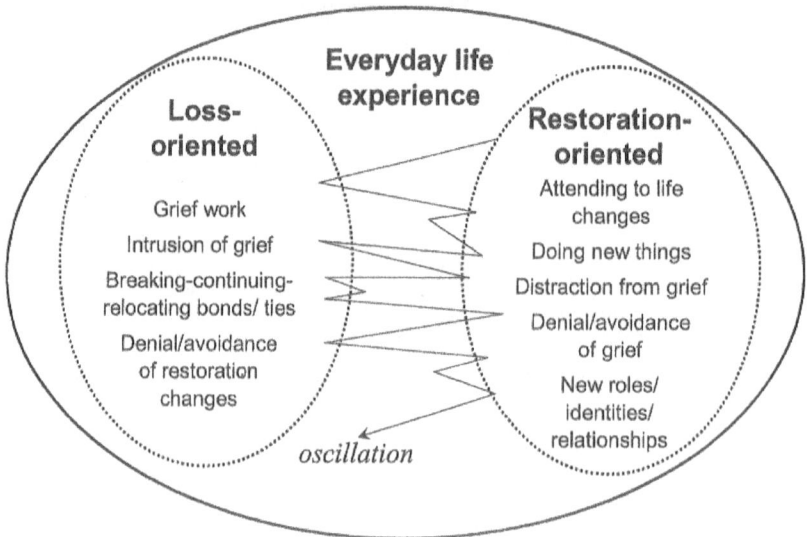

Everyday life experience

Loss-oriented

Grief work

Intrusion of grief

Breaking-continuing-relocating bonds/ ties

Denial/avoidance of restoration changes

Restoration-oriented

Attending to life changes

Doing new things

Distraction from grief

Denial/avoidance of grief

New roles/ identities/ relationships

oscillation

Grief Model
(Dr. John Brantner)

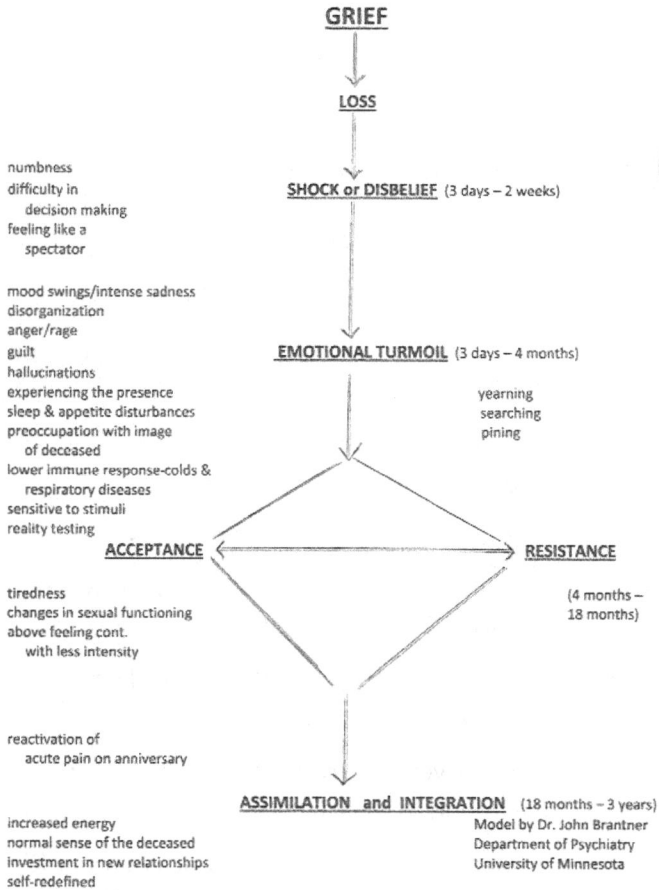

GRIEF

↓

LOSS

numbness
difficulty in
  decision making
feeling like a
  spectator

SHOCK or DISBELIEF (3 days – 2 weeks)

mood swings/intense sadness
disorganization
anger/rage
guilt
hallucinations
experiencing the presence
sleep & appetite disturbances
preoccupation with image
  of deceased
lower immune response-colds &
  respiratory diseases
sensitive to stimuli
reality testing

EMOTIONAL TURMOIL (3 days – 4 months)

yearning
searching
pining

ACCEPTANCE ⟵⟶ **RESISTANCE**

tiredness
changes in sexual functioning
above feeling cont.
  with less intensity

(4 months –
18 months)

reactivation of
  acute pain on anniversary

ASSIMILATION and INTEGRATION (18 months – 3 years)

increased energy
normal sense of the deceased
investment in new relationships
self-redefined

Model by Dr. John Brantner
Department of Psychiatry
University of Minnesota

Notes added from lecture
By Dr. Janice Winchester Nadeau, PhD.
Grief Therapist

Thirty-two Days from There to Here

August 31: Bob reported bleed. I pushed him to go to Emergency. Sinus infection diagnosed. I'm incredulous. I push Bob to make doctor's appointment

Appointment the following Wednesday.

September 1: Plans made to drive together to Amy and Lars' cabin.

September 2: We drive to cabin. We babysit the five grandchildren in the evening.

I notice Bob's lack of fine motor skills.

September 3: Bob loses temper at the cabin over insignificant direction. Big fight ensues.

September 4: We drive back to Twin Cities, no discussion of fight. Bob loses track of time.

September 5: Bob drives Sibley East Teachers to training from Arlington to Jordan, MN.

September 6: Mass is seen in Bob's head at Waconia-Ridgeview Hospital. His doctor orders him to report immediately to Abbott-Northwestern Hospital. He calls me for a ride. CAT scan at Abbott reveals brain tumor.

September 7: Bob has test to see if they can shut off an artery feeding the tumor—unsuccessful. Bob returns to my condo with me to stay the night.

September 8: I take Bob back to Arlington. He is to go home and stay there until the next Thursday.

September 11: Bob drives to bus garage. Makes arrangements for a sub bus driver for the time he will be in the hospital.

September 12: Bob drives to friends' house. Makes arrangements for friend to feed/water bull.

Bob drives to Glencoe to get ground corn for bull. Fills gas. Debit card will not work. Gas station will not accept check. Bob loses temper. Bob drives to get cash at bank in Arlington. Bob loses temper at bank.

September 13: Bob fills out necessary paperwork at bank as Lars has directed him.

Bob walks the fields picking up corn cobs for the bull.

September 14: I pick up Bob for first of two surgeries to be on Friday morning.

Bob speaks of death in indirect way on way to Twin Cities.

I make supper for the two of us.

Bob sleeps on my couch.

September 15: Bob has first surgery—tube placed in head to drain hydrocephalacy.

September 16: Bonnie flies in.

	Krista visits Bob at Abbott
	Bonnie and I visit Bob at Abbott.
September 17:	Krista, Bonnie, and Amy visit Bob at Abbott.
September 18:	Surgery to remove tumor takes entire day.
	Bonnie flies back to Indiana.
September 19:	Bob is awake in morning, signs to me, I misinterpret sign.
	I call Bob's sister.
	Brain scan reveals small bleed.
	Bob is intubated in the evening.
September 20:	Bob remains unconscious, on breathing tube.
	I go to Abbott in evening to see if Bob will recognize me, he does not.
	I call pastor.
September 21:	Bob is unconscious, on breathing tube.
	I am sure death is imminent.
	I do not go to Abbott.
September 22:	Bonnie gets call that Bob has tanked and makes call to remove breathing tube.
	Family meets at noon with pastor.
	Breathing tube is removed.
	Bob dies at 7:08 p.m.
	We decide to donate Bob's corneas.
	I call pastor that death has occurred.
	I complete paperwork for cornea donation.
September 23:	Mortuary picks up body.
	I buy cemetery plot.

I arrange for shipping of bull.

September 24: The family rests.

September 25: Bonnie flies in.

Bonnie, Krista, Amy, and I meet to plan agenda for Tuesday.

September 26: Planning for funeral at Kolden in Arlington, stops to find out about Bob's accounts. Paying for locks, stopping at motel, ordering flowers.

We stop at church to leave funeral service notes for pastor.

We stop at farm to check and obtain necessary paperwork, move vehicles.

September 27: I have doctor's appointment.

I write funeral sermon.

Shipper picks up bull with neighbors.

September 28: I have doctor's appointment.

I have blood transfusion.

September 29: I arrange and pack clothes for the weekend.

Amy, Lars, and family drive to Arlington.

September 30: We all meet at Zion Lutheran Church, the place of the funeral.

Visitation, funeral, lunch, and burial occur.

Cleaning begins at the farm.

October 1: Cleaning is finished at the farm.

Everyone returns home.

March 8, 2002

The Sale of the Dairy Cows

TWO EVENINGS AGO, my ex-spouse called me that the barn had been condemned, and that, because of the dirtiness of the barn and the farmyard, the creamery would no longer accept the milk the cows produced. In a panic, my husband had called another creamery, I think expecting a positive response from them, yet knowing that such a response would not be forthcoming unless he miraculously "cleaned up his act." He was crying, I could tell. And he asked if I could come for a few days, I don't really know what for—to get things cleaned up? An impossible task considering we are still experiencing winter, and the dirtiness of the barn, judging from my experience of the entire farmyard when I visited it last October to pick up a few belongings, was well out of hand.

Of course, I refused. And certainly, my schedule for some time ahead is full. I have put in a very busy couple of weeks at the church, and even at the time of our conversation, felt completely exhausted having hoped to catch an hour of rest between events, which was the reason I was home to even answer the call at all.

I calmly discussed with him the matter of selling the cows, which really was the only option open. He expressed his fear that, by tomorrow, the whole town would be talking about his failure. I calmly asked him if the "whole town" didn't already know the obvious. Others had phoned and expressed to me the concern over both Bob and his care of the farm on a few occasions. I had chosen not to act on their expressions of concern. After all, I had left the farm, the cows, and all the problems associated with Bob and them six years ago, having been divorced from it all now nearly four years.

I was surprised by my calm detachment in my conversation. Yet also, I was surprised by the depth of the feeling of loss that came to me from somewhere deep inside. The building of the barn, my husband's dream from as far back as I had known him, had been a big event—probably the biggest event of our marriage. It had also defined the entire nature and routine of our marriage, and had greatly influenced not only our lives, but our children's lives.

From the beginning of our marriage, everything had been defined in terms of the building of the barn. We had put off having a family, I had sacrificed both my children's care and safety and valuable time I could have spent with them as they grew up, because of the barn, its costs, and the requirements of time and energy put into making a go of it all once the barn was built. It was because of "the barn,' we did not begin our family until we had been married nearly four years. It was because of "the barn," we lived in abject poverty in the house. It was because of "the barn," that I went off birth control and accidentally became pregnant with our second child. It was into "the barn" that all of my husband's inheritance went. It was because of "the barn" that we faced seventeen-and-a-half percent interest rates during the 1980's, that for years we drove a car that was undependable and unreliable. I believe that it is because of "the barn" that the same carpet and drapes hang in the farmhouse today as the day we moved into it, the same drafty windows, the same old linoleum.

Time has a way of going by. The girls are grown. I have left the farm—left all of it behind. But the memories, good or bad, are still in there. They still define some twenty plus years of my life—years in which the days and weeks were framed by morning and evening milking of the cows and chores with the animals. Could I even count in my head the hours spent building fences, cleaning manure out of buildings, feeding baby calves—trying to get them to live beyond all odds? The freezing winter mornings when my toes would scream in frozen pain from having dealt with a major disaster related to taking care of the cows—a sick animal out in the shed, a frozen waterer, and electric fence that was not working. All for the sake of the cows—his dream.

It is over. The last of the herd will go to auction on Monday. I will not be there to see them go. But, somewhere deep inside, I will feel their going. Even though I am not there, and they are no longer a part of my life. I will feel the waste of the years I spent tending them, worrying about them, nursing them, struggling with them. Did you know that for most of those years each animal was personally named by me as they came from their mother's womb? I have seen both birth and death up close. The miracle when a newborn calf made its first cry. The swarming flies and open, starring eyes of those animals lost to disease or the elements.

I left it all behind six years ago, but now, it is finally over—at least this phase with the barn and the cows. Maybe the sale of the farm itself lies ahead. I ponder the day we signed the contract for deed. I walked on the driveway thinking, "This is our land now. It is really ours." My husband owes me a mortgage on the portion of it I claimed as mine in the divorce—just a fraction of its total worth.

The farmhouse, my house, lies in filth, trashed and dirty, cobwebs connecting curtain to corner to doorframe. The house cries of abandonment. It says, "a family once lived here." And I see in my mind the place clean and sparkling when company was coming. Or the lawn and yard clean shaven and orderly as the sun set in the west—as pretty as a park in July. My oldest daughter swinging and singing away in the warm March when she turned three. The figures of my children walk in the farm's shadows. In my mind, I hang out the wash in the warm summer breeze as the sweet smell of fresh cut alfalfa drifts by.

Yet, the memories of the barn, and the cows, and the house, and the children growing are overshadowed by the darkness of being beaten and abused, of hiding for fear of my life, of destruction and chaos, of family outings ending with an abusive episode, or a rainstorm being followed by a gash in my leg, or having my head beaten into the cement block wall, or the scarf I was wearing twisted around my neck until I couldn't get air. There is that dark place. It will neither go away nor will it become lighter. It is my history—part of who I am today.

And what was all of it for, I ask this day as the cows go to market, the barn stands in filth and disrepair, and the farmyard sleeps unkept under a shimmer of snow? "Do not store up your treasure on earth . . . "

www.ingramcontent.com/pod-product-compliance
Lightning Source LLC
Chambersburg PA
CBHW071346090426
42738CB00012B/3032